# WHERE
## THE HELL
## ARE YOU
# GOING?

## MINDFULNESS FOR
## THE RESTLESS SOUL

*Avi Raa*

## ACKNOWLEDGMENT

The whole universe has to come together to move a single blade of grass. This book would not have been possible without the support of everything that has ever happened. I am especially grateful to my students, who record, transcribe, edit, and publish my talks.

# TABLE OF CONTENTS

# INTRODUCTION

Heaven and hell, Avi contends, are not physical places, but the states of our mind. A centered and rooted mind, fully immersed in the present, embodies the essence of heaven. Conversely, a mind entangled in the past and future, disconnected from the now, resides in a self-imposed hell. Choosing to embrace the present moment is not just about adopting a mindful lifestyle, it's nothing short of choosing between life and death, for one can live nowhere else but in the present.

In this revolutionary and thought-provoking work, enlightened teacher Avi, drawing from his experiential journey into the depths of the present moment, introduces us to the mysterious realm of the "now," which he describes as the only reality of life. Through systematic and time-tested mindfulness techniques, he unveils the art of being here and now.

Avi's teachings embody the wisdom of the ages, demystifying the deceptively simple, yet easily misunderstood art of being present. He emphasizes that mindfulness isn't just a way of becoming more peaceful and joyful; it is also a direct path to enlightenment.

This book is Avi's compelling call to action, urging us to pause amidst our relentless pursuit of external goals. He asks us to slow down and reflect on the sheer magnanimity of the present moment, to which we have become oblivious.

This thought-provoking guidebook goes much deeper than the generally accepted superficial understanding of mindfulness, to drive home the point that mindfulness is not just about being in the present moment, but about using the present as a door to descend to the depths of your being.

Being in the present moment is not just about smelling the flowers and feeling your footsteps; it is a complete spiritual discipline that can take you to enlightenment - the ending of the cycle of birth and death. It is a gateway to heightened consciousness and unbridled bliss.

# CHAPTER ONE

# THERE IS NO INNER AND OUTER

*How do I access my inner being by watching my body? Isn't there a contradiction here?*

The whole idea of inner and outer is a purely human construct, just like heat and cold, light and darkness, good and bad. These are all perceptual labels. We experience something, and it gives us a certain sensation, which we then label. There is no one in existence recording these perceptions. Existence does not care about the difference between heat and cold, right and wrong, or good and bad - existence is supreme intelligence.

When intelligence reaches its peak, all labels disappear. Everything becomes part of the same realm. That is why reality is one, nature is one, and aliveness is one. You can always be sure of this. You can never wake up one day and realize a totally different self. You will always be you. At the deepest point of your being, the perception of the "I," the perception of the self, is unchanging. What you were when you were five years old will be the same when you are fifty or even five hundred. It does not matter. This lifetime or the next, no matter how many lifetimes you live, no matter how many times you come back to the same cycle of birth and death, your perception of the I is always the same. So is the perception of the I of all other creatures. Why? Because all other experiences of I are simply labels and extensions. "I did this." "I did that." "I feel good." "I feel bad." These are all human labels.

Similarly, "I am inside." "I am outside." What separates the inside from the outside? If you are inside something, are you not also, in some ways, outside as well? What separates the inside from the outside except for words? There is no one stopping you from going in and out except your own mental construct. It is the same with the body. The body is the door that is always open. Nobody is stopping you from going in or out, except for your definitions of what is inside and what is outside. "When should I go in and when should I go out?" For a moment, if you can assume that you are always inside, you will see that this whole idea that you need to go somewhere very far deep down inside you to connect with yourself is again, a perceptual labeling of the mind. Because the mind does not understand the nature of reality, it always seems like you have to go somewhere, and the mind loves going somewhere. It enjoys the idea of going places. What it hates the most is being here. So if you were to tell the mind - "Bliss is right here. Inside is right here. Aliveness is right here. Experience it." - it will ask for directions. In asking for directions, it is assumed that it has to go somewhere. By its very nature, the mind is movement. The mind is change. In the best-case scenario, it will circle around the truth, but it will never land on it.


## START WATCHING THE BODY

What happens when you start watching the body? You start exploring the door. You could be far away from the body. You could be in your dreamland - which is where you are most of the time - deeply asleep in your thoughts. If you are thirsty for awakening, if you yearn to know what it is to be truly awake - if you think life is so intoxicating and mesmerizing when you are asleep - just imagine how much more intoxicating it can be when you are awake. A desire should arise - "I want to taste that intoxication at least once before this body is given back to the maggots because I cannot hold on to it forever. I want to experience the truth. At this point, my only reality is my body, although I know that it is the most transient of entities, compared to eternity, compared to the depth of the present moment, or compared to how long eternity is. The body is so ephemeral, so transient. It is here now, and gone tomorrow."

In one blink of an eye, you take birth, you live, you grow up, you have all these sense pleasures and experiences, and in the next moment, it is gone. While you are going through the experience, it seems like it is long. "Oh, I am going to be in this body for a long time," because that is the mind holding on to that idea, the shadow of immortality. Because it is close to the self, it feels like it is going to be forever, and it adds that perception to the body. When you are alive, you never actually feel like you are going to die, although death could be lurking right there in the corner.

Death is always a part of life. We are never far from it. When it happens to you, you are always surprised. And it always happens too soon. I have heard stories of people dying in their nineties and their relatives saying, "We never expected that he would go so soon. He still had so much life in him." But what they are holding on to is life. They don't want to think about death. When it happens, it's always a surprise. But the body is already in the grave. One foot is already there.

Before the inevitable happens, if you have a desire to glimpse aliveness, to glimpse the true nature of your being, to wake up before you lose the opportunity, then do it because this life, this moment, is your guarantee. You never know what you will be in the next life. You never know how deep your unconsciousness will be in the next life. Unconsciousness is always deep. You have to crawl out of it. Look how long it has taken you to crawl out of your unconsciousness - to wake up, to realize the nature of your body, to start moving, to start learning how to speak, and then pick up scriptures and read and understand, and then come to this sense that there is a self, an inner and an outer and that you can move deeper and awaken. How long has it taken?

There has been no case of a child becoming enlightened - not a single case. After an individual becomes enlightened, we want to see that individual as special, so we add that special quality to their childhood and say, "He was enlightened all his life. He was like this when he was five." The stories of the Buddha are a beautiful example. It is said that when he was a child, a toddler, he was sitting under the shade of a mango tree while his family members were farming. The story tells that the shade of the mango tree never moved throughout the day, even though the sun moved. The shade was always on Buddha because the tree was protecting the boy. If the shade had moved, the boy would have been in the hot sun. This is a very apt example for a country like India, where shade is very important. You would probably not use the same story if the Buddha were to be born in America. But in India, it is a very good example.

We know that when he was a toddler, the Buddha was just a boy, he was just a baby - no different from any other baby. But we project our thoughts and desires onto him because that is our deep desire. Why? Why hasn't there been a single case of an individual becoming enlightened so early? It takes time to get out of unconsciousness. You have to become aware of your body, your mind, and your ego, and start questioning it. If all of that has happened in this life, then you are ripe for realization. Most people are ripe for realization because they have gone through that learning process. But for whatever reason, they give up on this life and say, "I will think about it in my next life. This life is for sense pleasures. This life is for accumulating wealth. This life is for being famous."

The desire to awaken should be a matter of life and death. Because it is a matter of life and death. When you awaken, you have found life. You have found the elixir of life. You have found the ocean of life. There is no death for you. Death is purely an imaginary concept for the one who is awakened. But for the one who is not awakened, death is always there. It is always looming as a shadow, and it is the single biggest source of frustration because you know somewhere deep down that death is not your nature.

But your body is moving closer and closer to death - everything around you is a reminder of death, and nothing scares you like death.

## CONNECT WITH YOUR TRUE SELF

All the fears that you experience, such as fear of insecurity, fear of losing something, and fear of something damaging your self-image, are part of the same fear: the fear of death. Awakening is a matter of life and death, but you cannot start with death. These are the only two realities of life: life and death, but you do not know what death is. You cannot begin your inquiry from death, so the only other option is to start from life.

Where is your life throbbing at its fullest? Where is your life pulsating in all its pristineness? In your body, not in your mind. In your mind, it is purely imagined. In your body, in the sensations of your body, in your breath, in the movement of your blood, in the movement of your muscles, every moment you are connected to aliveness. Not only are you connected to an individual phenomenon of aliveness, but you are also on an island of aliveness. There is so much aliveness there. There are so many things living there in your body. So much is happening there. You are right at the seat of aliveness. That's where you start.

How is it that watching the body can help you connect with your true self? The body is the seat of aliveness, and it is also the door. By watching your body, you start inquiring into the nature of the door. First, you understand it. You drop all the labels of inside and outside - all the sensations, all the sense pleasures. Slowly, when you are able to watch, all these things disappear and the door widens. As of now, you can see the door, but it is just a single point. By watching the body, that door slowly expands. It's the same body, but it gives way to the beyond. As it expands, you start believing that you can pass through it.

As of now, you are not even attempting because the body is so rigid. "There is no way I can break through this. There is no way I can break through my sense perceptions." The reason you are unable to break through is because you have not watched the body enough. The amount of time you have spent watching other things throughout your life - if you had spent even a fraction of that time watching your body - you would have been awakened by now. It is not the most difficult of things to do, but if you have not been watching, when you begin to watch your body, it will seem like a very alien concept.

Watching the body is the way, the door. But you cannot watch the body unless you make it your absolute most important, highest priority. And you cannot make it your highest priority unless it is a matter of life and death. Contemplate on death. Think about death, so you know that you have to move towards life. The aliveness that you are experiencing now is happening through the body, so it is not going to last. The body is allowing you to find the true aliveness before it can no longer give you directions. As of now, it is helping you in every which way possible. It is not happy. It knows it is in pain. It knows that it has to endure this experience of life. But why is it doing this? So that it can push you over the edge so you can fall into that ocean of life. But unless you are willing to jump, unless it becomes a matter of life and death, you will not be able to take the plunge.

## THE "FOWL-MOUTHED" PARROT

A man walks into a pet store and sees a parrot for sale. The parrot is expensive, but the man decides to buy it anyway. The parrot is delivered to the man's house and he quickly realizes that the parrot has a vulgar vocabulary. The man tries to teach the parrot some new words, but the parrot refuses to learn anything else.

One day, the man has had enough and decides to punish the parrot. He puts the parrot in the freezer for a few minutes, hoping that the cold temperature will teach the parrot a lesson. After a few minutes, the man takes the parrot out of the freezer and sets it on the counter. The parrot shivers and says, "I am sorry for my behavior. It won't ever happen again."

The man is amazed and asks, "How did you learn your lesson so quickly?"

The parrot replies, "May I ask what the chicken did?"

## CONTEMPLATING ON DEATH

Death is what scares us. Death is what makes us learn. Some of our most profound, intimate moments of learning that have become a part of us have happened because of the fear of death. Any learning that happens around the vicinity of the fear of death sticks. You will not have any trouble remembering it. You can forget most other things, but you cannot forget those moments when you came very close to death and what you learned from those moments.

Just like there is death in the physical realm, there is also death in the mental realm. Death cannot extend to the being, but it can extend to the mind and the body. You can contemplate on death by using your mind. When you are just entertaining thoughts of life and living - it's all about aliveness and living - you are in the mind. Because the mind is imaginary, you can strike a balance by adding a little bit of contemplation on death. Why? Because that much fear of death will make you watch life more consciously.

As of now, because there is no contemplation of death, you are not watching life. You are not watching it unfold. You are okay to just let the experience take you wherever it wants to take you because you are not seeing the end of the body. When you begin to see the end of the body, then you realize what a gift, what a blessing it is that you are alive and you have a body. This realization will allow you to experience aliveness in an entirely different way.

This body is going to be nothing in a few years. The only thing that will be remembered about you is your contemplation on aliveness. Whatever you created, whatever expressions that came out of that connectedness with your aliveness is what will remain. When you read a book, you most likely don't even know the body that has written the book. You don't know how that body looked or how it worked. Physicality is the least important thing. But when you are reading it, if whatever you are reading is resonating with you, you are feeling the aliveness of the person who is no longer here. They have left a trace of their aliveness, which has become immortal -

in a small expression of a book, a painting, or of anything they created. But it cannot happen without the body.

Look at the creative power that hides within you. A woman can give birth using the body. She can create life inside her. Why are we searching for God and creation in an existence outside of us? Where are human beings coming from? They are not dropping from heaven. They are coming from inside us. We have the potential to create. If we can create another human being, if a man can contribute to the creation of another human being, if a woman can be a womb to create another human being, what is the necessity for a separate creator? What is the necessity for heaven and hell? What is the necessity for all the theological mental gymnastics? It is pure distraction.

Whatever it is that your scriptures are promising you after death, you can experience it right here, right now, if you use the body as the door. Start with the body because the body is also inside. The whole idea that the body is outside and "I need to travel inside" is a contradiction. It is purely imaginary, because the body is an extension of the mind, and the mind is also an extension of the being. Everything is swimming in the same ocean of consciousness. You have to start somewhere, so start with the body.

## CHAPTER TWO

# DON'T GET CARRIED AWAY

Let's explore a mindfulness technique of watching your sense pleasures. Firstly, you have to look at your senses and the desires of your senses as something very fundamental to your being. There cannot be any feelings of guilt or rejection toward your senses. This is the hard part because we have been conditioned for a very long time to look at the sense pleasures of the body as something negative, as something that has to be suppressed, conquered, and controlled.

When we are talking about sense pleasures, we're not just talking about our desire to see beautiful things, hear melodious sounds, taste nice things, or even the desire for sex. All this is external. What is more important is the force, the energy that is finding its expression in all these different dimensions of life. And this energy is not against life. Not only is it not against life, it emanates from life. Look at all the creatures of existence. Sense pleasure is what drives them, what moves them.

It is through sense pleasures that we take birth. It is in pursuit of our sense pleasures that we live. Eventually, the waning of the energy that is necessary to experience all that our senses want us to experience is what we recognize as the death of the body. The body becomes weak. It is no longer pursuing those sense pleasures with the same ferocity, with the same enthusiasm and desire. That's what old age and death are. So, the pursuit of sense pleasures is the primary driving force of life. That is why there's a deep connection between how you experience life on the outside and how you feel it inside. Our senses take the experience of life and transmute it into something different. This transformation happens inside us.

We don't experience life as just a combination of colors, smells, or sounds. When our senses pick up these experiences and put them inside, they transform into something else. They transform into an experience - an experience that gives us immense joy, and immense pleasure, and can even connect us to deeper states of bliss. So the first thing to recognize in watching our sense pleasures is to embrace the idea of watching them. If you watch them with guilt, you're already filtering it through your conditioning. Then the watching is not pure. It is intermixed with too many thoughts.

## EMBRACING SEX

Let's take the example of the pinnacle of our sense pleasures, which is the desire for sex. When the desire arises in you, you have choices: You can engage in that desire, you can watch the source of that desire, and not worry too much about the source, just jump into action. This is the normal process of the mind - it is attracted to something and it moves toward it. Let's say you see a beautiful person. There is a desire to connect, and you act upon it. You have a conversation with them. What you do from that point onwards when that sense pleasure arises - is the action.

Another thing you can do is suppress it. The moment the thought arises, you feel guilty. "Oh, I should not be having these thoughts. These thoughts are sin. These thoughts are negative. Let me not think about it. Let me divert my attention." That is what people have been taught to do. It has been more than two thousand years since the tale of the Garden of Eden, and Man has still not gotten over the guilt of experiencing one of the most basic fundamental driving forces of life, which is the desire for procreation, for sex, for sense pleasures. Sex is simply the pinnacle of sense pleasures because all the senses come together. Your visual sense, your listening sense, your smell, taste, and touch - everything comes together in sex. That is why the draw and desire are maximum. But it is the same desire we see in our separate senses when we look at something beautiful, when we experience something pleasant inside. The sensations of feeling, tasting, or hearing are independent, but when they all come together, they come together to give us an experience of something beyond.

If we approach the primary desire of life with guilt, then that guilt is bound to trickle down to all other dimensions of life. With one look at the human race, we can see that is exactly what has happened. Man is guilty of all kinds of pleasures, and not only sex because that is the primary pleasure. When you condemn that primary pleasure - and it is such a basic dimension of life that affects every other dimension of life - then naturally, you're condemning everything beautiful, everything pleasant. You are eventually condemning the highest possible experience: the experience of undivided bliss.

What do you experience at the pinnacle of sex? You're not experiencing the other person. You're not experiencing your body or the other person's body. You're not experiencing your mind or another mind. In that moment of orgasm, in that moment of experiencing the pinnacle of your energies reaching that climax, you are aware of nothing. In that single moment, your body consciousness is gone. Your mental consciousness is gone. Your awareness of the place where you are, your name, your form, how famous you are, how rich you are, which religion you belong to - everything is gone. I am certain that a Hindu experiences orgasm the same way a Christian or a Muslim experiences it. Religion doesn't even go there. Religion has no place there because it is true. It is real.

You can talk on the outside. You can create theories. You can have layers upon layers of theology on God, the Son, the Holy Ghost, on this and that, but when it comes to experience, talk is just talk. Why? Because life does not listen to all that nonsense. The mind listens to it - the mind contemplates all. The mind can be fooled, but your being cannot be fooled. Your being knows what you want. Your being knows that you are a creature of bliss and that is what you're striving for. Your mind can get confused. Your mind can sometimes follow a religion. It can follow different paths - it can be tricked. The promise of a shortcut can trick it. "If only I do this. If only I believe in this, follow the son of God, read the Quran, or follow the Gita, I'm gonna get there." These are shortcuts, which are for the mind. For your body, for your being, there is no shortcut. There is only one shortcut for your being to experience bliss, and that is sex, which is the pinnacle of sense pleasures.

## YOU DESERVE BLISS

The first thing is to approach the life force that is animating you with a sense of reverence - with a sense of divine reverence - to look at bliss as something that you deserve, not as something that you have to experience with a sense of guilt. Once that is clear, then all the other sense experiences are part of that same divine nature. Watching sense pleasures is to crave beautiful experiences and watch them without getting submerged in them. That is the art. First is the recognition of sense pleasures as your fundamental nature without any guilt, and the second is to watch them without getting completely engulfed - without getting completely lost.

Why is it important to not get lost? If you want to extend that one single momentary pleasure more than a moment, then you need to watch it. It is only in watching that you can separate yourself from the experience and prolong it. Another beautiful thing happens when you make a conscious effort to prolong the experience - you will learn the art of connecting to that experience even without the direct need for it. You can experience the same pleasure of sex inside without the actual need for sex. That's what going deeper into meditation is. That's what going higher is. That's what transcendental experience is - what enlightenment is. Enlightenment is a moment where you are totally in that other dimension of life. You are in bliss without the body to pull you back immediately.

The only difference in all of the sense pleasures is that the body eventually pulls us back. You want to eat something really tasty. You cook it, serve yourself, and begin to eat. Now, how long does the pleasure last? It lasts only as long as the food is in your mouth. If you try to recreate that experience without food, you cannot. It's the same with looking at a sunset. You're watching a beautiful sunset. How long does that experience last? Within a matter of a few minutes that experience is gone. And then when you come back home, if you try to recollect that experience and try to experience that same sense of bliss and joy, you cannot. You will only recollect it as a memory. It's the same with sex. You could have had the best sexual experience, but when you're sitting and thinking about it, reflecting on it, you're not having an orgasmic experience. You're not experiencing bliss. You're only thinking about it. It's only part of the mind. Why? Because you are still dependent on sense pleasures.

Watching sense pleasures is to identify all these desires that are arising in us and try to see if we can replicate that experience without the experience. So, if you are sitting on a mountain top looking at a beautiful sunset, be aware, be alert, not just to the experience of the sunset, but to the experience of you experiencing the sunset. That is the trick. It is to watch the one who's watching and stay in that moment for as long as you can without forgetting the watcher. And then when the sun disappears, at that very moment you feel, "I'm missing this experience," just close your eyes and try to hold on to that whole experience. Not of the sunset, but of the one who experienced the sunset.

The trick is that there is someone who can experience unlimited bliss. That someone is what you are trying to recognize. As of now, your mind is standing as a barricade between you and your sense pleasures. By practicing the art of watching your mind, watching where your sense pleasures arise from, how are they moving, and what kind of changes they are creating in your body, you can direct them. Instead of those sense pleasures going out, you can turn them around and move them inward. You must pay attention to what's happening. You mustn't forget what is happening in the present moment.

There is no other source of our chaos and confusion in life - we do things unconsciously when our senses are intoxicated by anything. There is a beautiful Zen saying: "Too much color blinds the eye. Too much sound deafens the ear. Too much taste dulls the tongue." Why? What is the limiting factor? Why should too much sense pleasure dull the mind, or dull the body? Because you're experiencing bliss, it has to be something natural, and yet at the same time, why does it eventually numb your senses? This is important to understand.

## SEEING WITH THE "I" - NOT THE EYE

Too much color indeed dulls your visual senses. But what the Zen saying is talking about is not the dulling of your physical senses, but there is something behind all these senses which is much purer. If you can see this much with your eyes, you can see ten times this much from the "I" that is behind the eye. If you can taste this much using your tongue, you can taste ten times more using your inner being. As of now, we are experiencing life in a limited way using each one of our senses. When we can experience life directly from the present moment, without this filtering mechanism, then the experience is complete and doesn't leave any residue.

Our senses are always intoxicated. Our eyes are always intoxicated with color. Our taste buds are always intoxicated with some taste. If you pay attention and observe each one of your senses, - seeing, smelling, tasting, touching, and hearing, they're always in some form of intoxication. You can experience this when you eat. Immediately after eating, you will feel a sense of drowsiness. Where does this drowsiness come from? Your senses are being intoxicated by the food. And if you pay even closer attention, everything intoxicates you. And when you take that intoxication to its extreme level with alcohol, drugs, or something else, that's when your senses are fully submerged.

What happens when you're drunk? Your ability to perceive reality as it is gets distorted. That is, in a way, what is happening through our senses. The perception is happening, but we are unable to let go of it and connect with something pure inside. Intoxication is fine, as long as there is a way to step out of it. When you drink and become intoxicated, you are not bothered about it too much because you know that sooner or later, the intoxication will wear off and you will come back to your normal state of being. If I were to tell you, "Here is a drink. Once you drink this, you will always be intoxicated. There's no way to come back to a normal state of consciousness." You will never touch that drink. Why do you want to be intoxicated all the time? I'm not talking about intoxication in some divine sense. Just be drunk. Why would you want to be drunk all the time? You know you cannot move properly, you cannot think or act properly, but still, you indulge in it because you know that it's only momentary. It is a momentary numbing of the senses, and eventually you come back.

What if I were to tell you that all the sense pleasures you're experiencing are a kind of intoxication? Life itself is an intoxication. There is a way to step out of it. There is a way to move beyond. Would you not pursue that path? If there is a way, even for a single moment, for you to step out of the intoxication of life, and perceive life in all its purity, the difference would be exactly like this - the difference between your normal state of consciousness and your inappropriate drunken state of consciousness. You can just picture yourself the way you move, the way you think, the way you speak, when you're drunk, and when you're not. That much is the difference between what we call a normal state of consciousness and experiencing life in all its purity.

Humanity is in a confused mess because it is intoxicated, simply believing that it knows what it's doing. But deep down, unconsciousness and intoxication are driving the human race. We see anger, pain, frustration, violence, and all kinds of nonsense because people are moving about drunk.

## DRUNK AND CONFUSED

A man walks into a bar and orders a drink. He notices a jar full of money on the counter and asks the bartender what it's for. The bartender replies, "It's for a contest we are having. If you can complete three challenges, you win the money. The man is intrigued and asks what the challenges are. The bartender explains. First, you have to drink a whole gallon of pepper tequila. Then you have to go outside and remove a sore tooth from a mean alligator. Finally, there's a woman upstairs who's never had an orgasm - you have to give her one."

The man is hesitant but decides to give it a shot. He drinks the gallon of pepper tequila, which makes him incredibly sick. He stumbles outside and everyone hears a lot of commotion followed by the man yelling in pain. Finally, he stumbles back into the bar, covered in blood and scratches. He looks at the bartender and says, "Alright, where's the woman with the sore tooth?"

Watch yourself. Watch what you're doing. Pay attention to your senses. Senses can be intoxicated. They can be dulled to a point where what you think is normal might be far from normal. What you are experiencing as normal states of pleasure, displeasure, pain, frustration, rejection, and dejection are not normal at all. You are a creature of light. You are a creature of aliveness. You are a creature of bliss. Bliss is your original nature. You have to keep watching all your sense pleasures until each one of them transforms into bliss, until you are rooted in bliss, until you are rooted in the present moment.

## KEEP COMING BACK

Ask yourself these questions: How many times have you drifted in thoughts? How many times have you traveled in the vast landscape of your mind? How many different ideas have you entertained? How many different fantasies have you imagined? Why do you always come back? Why do you always come back to the present moment? If the present is not your true home, who is motivating you? Who's pushing you to come back? We keep thinking about it - it is so hard to be in the present moment. But at the same time, we fail to realize it is hard not to be in the present moment as well. Where do we go? Something throws us back to the present moment. Something always puts us back here and says, "Watch what's happening here." Some part of us knows that only the present moment is real - tomorrow is purely imagined.

You can live in all kinds of fantasies. You can be worrying about all the things that might happen or might not happen, or you could be reflecting on all the things you should have or you should not have done. But the reality is this moment. That is why you always come back to the present. You have lived long enough to know that there is something special here in the present moment. Hence, the reflection, "That is why I keep coming back. Even without my knowledge, even if I want to get lost, something is not allowing me to get lost. Something is reminding me to come back. Maybe I need to make a conscious effort to come back, instead of just leaving it for chance. When do I come back? How much do I come back? Let me make a conscious choice."

That's what mindfulness is. And mindfulness on sense pleasures is just to be aware that your sense pleasures are there to take you away. Watch them without any guilt - without any past conditioning. Enjoy them. Immerse yourself in your sense pleasures, but never forget the one who's experiencing. Never forget the one who's going through all the experiences. Then slowly, you will know what bliss is, independent of all sense pleasures. Then you can sit on a barren rock in the middle of nowhere, with no images, no experiences, and you will be blissed out both inside and out. You don't have to crave sex. You don't have to crave for sense pleasures. You don't have to keep on torturing yourself that you are unable to control your desires - you're unable to control your sense pleasures. This "controlling" is a useless word. You cannot control your sense pleasures. It is like trying to swim upstream. You cannot. Instead of controlling it, just observe it, and understand it, and therein lies the transcendence.

Where the Hell are you Going?

## CHAPTER THREE

# MY HEAD IS EXPLODING

*Why do I feel like my head is going to explode when I try to sit and watch my breath? How do I get over this initial terror?*

When you experience discomfort while trying to be mindful, it is a good sign. It is an indication that something is happening, something is changing. On the contrary - if you have just begun your mindfulness practice and it has only been, let's say, a few days since you started the practice and you're doing it effortlessly - you hardly have to think about it. Become skeptical. Become doubtful. Why? Because something should happen when you begin to watch yourself. Because you've not done it, it is not a part of your regular flow of life - it has to create disturbance. It has to make you feel like your head is going to explode. That is the way. That is the natural progression of understanding.

When you begin, the process is so new, so alien, that your mind begins to tremble. Because mindfulness is the slow erosion of the mind, the deeper you go into mindfulness, the more rooted you become in the present moment, and the less powerful and influential your mind becomes. The mind is a control freak - it has believed all along that it is the master of your being. It has been sitting on the throne like a king, commanding, ordering, and controlling - "Yes. Do this. No. Don't do that." The mind has not allowed anything to pass by without its permission. It has been the arbitrator, the ultimate arbitrator. You have been a servant to the mind. Anything you want to experience, anything you want to understand about life and yourself, you have taken it to the mind and asked its permission. "Is this right? Is this wrong? Should I do this? Should I not do this?"

## CONFRONTING THE EGO

Now, for the first time, you're doing something that does not require the interference of the mind. It's like all your life when you walked in front of the king, you bowed to him and paid your respect. Now suddenly you're walking without a care that he's sitting there. His head will explode. It has to explode. His ego has to tremble. "What is this? What is happening here? This is my world. This is my kingdom. I need to be in control of everything. What is this new thing? I cannot even see it. This creature is calling it silence, stillness, being in the present moment - what are these things? Get back to normal. Get back to paying your respects. Come to me asking for directions because you don't know anything. You cannot walk on your own. You cannot move on your own. You have to come to me. Otherwise, you're going to fall into a ditch. If you don't take my instructions, whatever path you're taking, this silence and stillness are going to take you into some dark corner and leave you there. Somebody has tricked your mind. Somebody has tricked you. Come back to me."

That's the screaming of the mind. Those arguments of the mind - the fear of the mind is what you are experiencing as an explosion inside. Otherwise, what is the necessity for an explosion? What is the need to feel agitated? Mindfulness is not something that is being added to your being. Why should your head explode? It is important to understand this explosion.

You have not added anything to the mind. You've not added a new ideology, or philosophy, or introduced a new concept into the mind for it to be disturbed. You are allowing the mind to be itself again. You are not trying to change minds. For example, when you are angry, mindfulness asks you to watch the anger, not go and change it - not try to find out the reason for the anger or feel guilty that you became angry - you aren't trying to do any of that. You are letting the mind be itself, letting emotions come and go, letting your judgments come and go. Mindfulness is just watching and observing what's happening without interfering with it. There is no reason for the mind to be agitated.

Where is this explosion coming from? Where is this disturbance coming from? There is another part of the mind that exerts its influence on every single dimension of life, yet when you inquire into the nature of its reality, it disappears. That is the ego. The ego has no basis in reality. You will not be able to bring out your ego and show it to people. You will not be able to stand in front of the mirror and look at your ego because it's not a thought process. If it is a thought process, you can recognize it. "Oh, this is a thought process. Let me do something with it." If it is physical, like the body, you can observe it. So, it is neither subtle like thoughts nor gross like the body. And yet, it is very real. That is what is exploding. The ego is what is being disturbed.

You've not added anything to the body or the mind, but you have added something to the ego. You've added silence. You've added stillness. What are these things? When you become silent, when you become still, and when you come back to the present moment, you cannot do things automatically anymore because the present moment is so intelligent, so aware, and so deeply rooted in life that it does not allow repetition. The present moment is so fresh and new that even if you're performing the same action when you begin to watch it, the way you perform it changes. Something changes in the way you move. Something changes in the way you speak. Something changes in the way you see. Why?

## WAIT FOR IT

Up until now, your "doing" was just an automatic mechanism that was going on. Your body was doing its thing, your mind was doing its thing, and the ego was satisfied. Now, your body is pausing. Your mind is pausing. Not because it does not want to perform those actions, but because it is experiencing a sense of newness. That is what you've added - and this is not added to the body or the mind. It is added to the ego, and because the ego is pure monotony, an automatic process, it has no pause. Ego is most powerful when it is allowed to run in automatic mode. The ego has different buttons - anger, happiness, sadness, and depression. What the ego wants you to do is just push the button and step away. It does not want you to interfere. It wants you to push the anger button and sit and watch that unfolding of anger, that unconsciousness, that movement, that alteration of the breathing, those thought processes. That is what the ego wants. Ego does not want you to control all these things - it wants you to leave it alone. That is the strength of the ego. Unconsciousness is the strength of the ego.

When you introduce mindfulness, you are directly questioning this monotonous, automatic mode of the ego that it has been in all its life. For the first time, you're telling it not to walk unconsciously - watch your walk. Now what happens when the watcher comes? The ego has to tremble. The ego is an extension of the mind. You will experience it as trembling in your mind - your mind is disturbed. But in reality, it's not even your mind, because eventually, your mind will settle down. With a little bit of practice, your mind will understand what's happening.

Your mind trembles only when it is unable to understand something, but the ego trembles for many different reasons - not just because it is unable to understand. The ego trembles when it sees its death - any sign, any indication, that something far superior is entering, and its job might be done.

When you try to find the ego, it is nowhere to be found. Nobody has ever found the ego. Nobody has ever had a conversation with the ego, but the ego is what has been driving their lives. It is what has been driving their ambitions and desires; it is what has been driving them crazy as well. Ego not only drives your life, it drives you crazy because it has no basis in reality. And yet, it has tremendous power over you.

When you become aware you are, in a way, signaling to the ego that "The beginning of your end has started." It is natural for the ego to feel as if everything is exploding. "My whole world is exploding. Everything I had so carefully constructed in my darkroom is now coming to light. I don't like light. I don't want to be seen. I am the ugliest creature in the whole universe, and I have hidden that. I have convinced this creature that ego is helpful - ego is beneficial. If light comes in and if I am revealed in all my imperfections, in all my ugliness, then what's going to happen to me?"

That's what mindfulness is. When you become mindful, you are putting a light on the ego - the darkest, the ugliest, the most illogical and insane part of us. If you remove the ego, everything is alive and bubbling. When the ego goes away, the mind becomes intelligent and illuminated. It looks at experiences differently. It looks at people differently. Every moment becomes a celebration because the mind is, by its very nature, illuminated by the self. It is the ego that instructs the mind to do certain things - "Go into automatic mode. Don't pause. Don't think when you get angry; just explode in anger. When you experience happiness, just become happy. Don't think about anything else."

This unconsciousness is what has been pushing us from one extreme experience to another. Ego doesn't understand the middle. It's not allowing us to be in the middle. Ego wants us to always be at the extremes because that is an automatic process. You get angry for no reason. You become happy for no reason. You get frustrated for no reason. You become depressed for no reason, and your ego loves all this. Mindfulness is poison for the ego. It dissolves the ego. For the first time, you're taking control of your mind and body away from the automatic processes of the ego and giving it to the conscious self. It is a beautiful process. It is a magical process that is happening. Your head should explode more. Your being should tremble more, and you should rejoice in it.

## DIGGING DEEPER TO FIND YOUR SELF

Every time you try to be mindful and you feel disturbed, some unknown happiness should take over. You should know that somebody is disturbed here, but it is not you. You don't have to take all the disturbances that are happening inside your being as disturbances that are happening to you, because you have multiple components. You have the body, the mind, the ego, and your self. The self can never be disturbed - it is always calm and relaxed. So there's always a part of you that is never disturbed.

When you dig a little deeper and observe your being, there is a part of you - even when your whole world is crumbling - that is untouched by any of that. That is the part of you that brings you back from chaos. Every time you've gone into the deep, dark corners of life, what has brought you back? If there was no independent entity that is separate from your mind, if there was no self that is always calm and relaxed, then there is no way you could have come back from all those moments. And there's no way people would have come back from all the experiences that they've gone through. They would get stuck in their experiences. They would fall into their emotional traps and get completely lost.

People can pull themselves back despite the power of the ego and the power of the mind because of this part of them that is never disturbed. Every other part of you is susceptible to disturbance; however, disturbances in those dimensions don't always indicate something is wrong - disturbance can also be a sign of transformation.

Disturbance in the body? No. It's not always bad. Sometimes the body is healing. It is going through certain processes. Because we don't see all the processes of the body when we are in pain, we complain. Yes, it is painful. Yes, it is difficult to experience that pain. But that pain is happening to the body. There has to be a detachment. These are the moments when you need to fall back on your self more. The closer you are to the body, the more attached you are to the body, the more pain, the more suffering.

Similarly, with the mind. The more you are attached to the desires of the mind, the more disturbed the thought processes. But again, not all disturbances of the mind are negative. Sometimes the mind figures things out. It is rearranging things. And any transformation, when it's happening, is painful. It is natural. If you've thrown things in your house here and there without a care - and you've been doing that all your life - suddenly, one day you wake up to that reality. You look at your house and say, "What a mess this is. Let me clean it up." What happens when you're cleaning it? There's no joy in cleaning it. You have to look at all the mess. You have to clean it. You've not cleaned it for such a long time, and now you're doing it for the first time. It is painful. It is disturbing. The mind is agitated by change because it prefers familiarity. It doesn't matter whether the change is good or bad, the mind enjoys familiarity.

Disturbances are natural in the body and the mind, and in the ego, it is even more natural, because the ego has no basis in reality. At least the mind has deep-rooted memories attached to it - it has a little bit of sense to it. The body has deep-rooted experiences. It has accumulated itself through an intelligent process.

The ego wakes up with you in the morning and dies in the night. And it again wakes up in the morning. It has no continuity - it is just like a ghost that comes and goes. So it's natural for the ego to become disturbed, especially when you are introduced to something so pure and transformative like mindfulness. Rejoice in the disturbance. Rejoice in the explosion. It is a sign that something grand is happening - something big is happening. Think about it: If such a small thing as watching the breath can disturb you, how much you should rejoice in that disturbance! If silence is added to your being, if stillness is added to your being, and if that is causing disturbance, you should rejoice in it. It takes a little bit of intelligence and a different way of looking at it.

## SHIFTING OF THE CENTER

Soon, the ego will understand. "I have to live with this. I have to make space for the present moment." Slowly, it will start moving to the side. Before, it was right at the center of your life. When the ego is at the center of your life, you can't even add one moment of silence to your being or it will rebel, it will tremble, but just keep on adding. Watch it tremble. Add more silence. The bigger the explosion, add more to it. Let the ego burn. Put fuel on that fire. Add more silence. More stillness. Become more aware. Let the ego cry. Let it tremble. Eventually, it will understand, and move to the side. That is all that is needed. If the ego moves to the side, then your centering has shifted, and your center is no longer the ego. You don't even have to eliminate the ego. You only have to move it away from the center for your true being, your true self - which has always been there, just covered up by the ego - to show itself again.

Once you become rooted in the present moment, once you become rooted in yourself, you can accommodate the ego. You can accommodate the mind. You can accommodate the body. All these things become experiences. The pain of the ego, the pain of the mind, the suffering of the body - these are all experiences. They are happening around the center. The way you experience life after that centering will be different from how you were experiencing life before that centering. Before the centering, every disturbance was yours. When the body was in pain, you were in pain. When the mind was in pain, you were in pain. When your ego was suffering, you were suffering. There's no separation at all.

Think about how absolute your suffering was, and now your center can never suffer. Suffering is not in its nature. The present moment cannot suffer. The self cannot suffer. Once you become rooted in the center, you can watch the processes of the mind, the body, and the ego - without getting lost in them. What a blessing it is to watch your mind without having to jump into it. What a blessing it is to watch the suffering of your body without becoming the suffering. And what a way to live. When your mindfulness extends to meditation and you start going deeper, the center will extend to a point where your ego will be pushed so far to the corner that it will be immaterial whether it's there or not. Eventually, it will be pushed out. In the moment of awakening, the ego goes away. Then your center has become your entire being. That is the ultimate objective of mindful meditation. As of now, you're trying to introduce the center of your being, so there's going to be disruption. There's going to be an explosion. Rejoice in it.

Where the Hell are you Going?

# CHAPTER FOUR

# WATCH THE WATCHER

*Yesterday, you talked about mindfulness and watching your breath. How can you continue with the process if you're not able to watch your breath? Okay. I mean, I can watch it for fifteen seconds, and it's gone. It's a constant battle.*

The difficulty in mindfulness is not the practice - it is not the complexity nor the mystery of the practice. It is not that sometimes you get it, sometimes you don't get it, sometimes you understand what mindfulness is, and sometimes you don't get it at all. None of these complications exist. By its very nature, mindfulness is simple. Watch the watcher. Watch the watcher. That's what mindfulness is. Consciousness is two-directional, but we are only familiar with one direction. Because we have been living unconsciously and subconsciously, most of our thought processes and activities have been happening without our permission. We only acknowledge them and watch them once in a while.

Most of what we do happens without our knowledge, but still, there is a memory of what's happening. Even when you don't watch what you're doing, at the end of the activity, you can still remember that you did that activity. Even if you didn't want to remember your walk, there's a part of you that is remembering it. This is one direction of consciousness - autonomous memory - which remembers everything.

This is where mindfulness gets a little tricky because remembering is already happening. Watching is already happening. When you try to watch something consciously, there is a sense of confusion as to "What am I doing in addition? What is this new kind of watching? What am I doing differently?" It is only when you start watching that you uncover the new dimension of watchfulness, which is in a completely different direction.

## YOUR MIND IS A FILTER

Consciousness is two-directional. One is observation of the action - observation of the object. Whatever it is you're observing, your consciousness is picking up that experience filtered through the mind. No experience from the outer world directly goes to the consciousness - the mind is always there as a filter. This is what we recognize as memory, cognition, our ability to remember things, and, to a certain extent, self-awareness. But the other dimension, the other direction that is hidden from us, is a connection between yourself and the outermost layer of perception, which has nothing to do with the mind. There is something that connects your innermost self and your outermost experience without the interference of the mind, without the constant conversation of the mind - you simply know the presence of something.

For example, if you were to be looking at two pots, when you watch with your mind, you can only watch one pot at a time with complete awareness of what's happening there. You cannot watch two pots. Why? Because when you're watching one pot, your focus is on that pot. When you're watching the other pot as well, your focus is now divided. When your focus is divided, it needs two moments to capture the same experience. It cannot do it at the same moment. You can only watch one pot. And however minuscule that time is, there is a time lag between your cognition shifting from that one pot to the other pot because the mind can only observe one thing at a time.

The mind is unidirectional - it is not multidirectional. We are used to focusing, not being aware, and we have mistaken focusing for awareness. When we watch something, we are actually focusing because, for us, watching is an effort. It is a conscious act, and it is being done through the mind, so you can watch one pot without any problem. You can just focus on it, and you only need one moment. But if you want to watch both pots together, the only way you can do so is by just looking at everything that is in the area of the pots without focusing on anything in particular.

Your mind picks up a lot of things. In that process, it also picked up the pot. It picked up the color of the pot. It picked up the shape and size of the pot. It picked up the floor on which it was sitting. But here is the difference: When you are watching one pot, it is possible to watch only that pot. You can forget all the other things. You can be completely blind to everything else, and you can only watch part of it. But when you decide to watch two things at the same time, you inevitably become aware of everything in between and surrounding them as well.

Awareness and mindfulness are entirely different from each other. Although focusing is important, it is only a small part of mindfulness. Mindfulness seems challenging because we confuse focus with awareness. The questions are, "When I'm focusing on this, how can I do that? When I'm focusing on my breath, how can I drive? How can I cook?" Yes, there is a contradiction there.

Let's say you are trying to focus on the breath - imagine you're reading a book. If I were to tell you to be watchful of your breath and you started focusing on the breath, how would you be able to read unless you were continuously going back and forth because your mind is limited in its ability to perceive multiple things? It can only perceive one thing at a time. It cannot perceive both the breath and what you're reading at the same time. If you were to tell the mind to watch the breath as well as to focus on reading, it would only keep going back and forth. Sometimes it's lost in the book - sometimes it's lost in the breath because the mind knows no other way of perceiving.

The only way the mind knows how to perceive something is to completely jump into that experience. The mind does not know how to sit on the fence and watch. If you were to point to something and say, "Watch that," it would immediately jump off the fence and go to it. And then, if you say, "What are you doing? I just want you to watch it." From here, the mind will come back running. It will forget that object. And then you question, "Why did you forget that object?" "Oh, I'm sorry. Let me go back again." That's what the mind is. The mind does not understand awareness. It doesn't even believe that it's possible to be aware of multiple things at the same time, because the mind is a one-way arrow. Once you shoot it, the arrow can only go in one direction. It cannot come back.

## MINDFULNESS COMES FROM THE SELF

Here is the most important thing to remember: Mindfulness has nothing to do with the mind. Mindfulness is not watching through the mind. It is watching through the self. It is watching through consciousness, through aliveness. It is watching through your being. There is another watcher, much bigger, much more powerful, much more capable, and much more intelligent, who knows no limitations. He's inside you, not inside your mind. The mind is simply an extension of the self - a tiny extension. When you're performing an activity and that activity requires you to focus, you use your mind.

When you began practicing mindfulness, you were taught to watch the breath, so you also tend to think mindfulness is about keeping your focus on the breath. Just like you're focusing on walking, eating, or driving, you think, "I need to focus on my breath as well." That is how it starts, and that is where the confusion is. When you start watching your breath, you cannot do other activities. When you're doing some other activity, you cannot watch your breath.

This is where you find it very challenging. "Why is it that I'm not able to do both things at the same time?"

It will take some time. You will constantly be going back and forth. And then eventually, you will realize the reason you're not able to do both is because you're disturbed. You're not relaxed enough. You are right at the surface of cognition. You have to go a little deeper. You've got to settle a little more into your being. On the surface, there's no way to perceive two things together. You can only go back and forth, and that's what is happening. But after some time, you understand there is another way of perceiving, which is, "When I relax more, I don't have to focus on the breath. I don't even have to focus on what I'm doing."

There is something so subtle and gentle - even one thought disturbs it. If you add anything more to that awareness, by saying, "Watch more closely, watch more intensely, you're not watching, do it correctly" - the mind is jumping in. When you're not doing any of this - when you're not agitating your consciousness, when you're not disturbing it, when you're relaxed - you can see that there is an underlying realm of awareness that is aware of everything automatically, whether you want it or not.

Mindfulness is about watching everything from that platform of awareness. So the deeper your relaxation, the easier it is to watch. That is why mindfulness is extraordinarily hard when you begin. It is one of the hardest things to do because it takes time to understand what we're trying to do. It's natural for us to slip into the mental grooves and do things just the way we've been doing them with the mind - focusing. But mindfulness is not focusing. Mindfulness is about being aware. Awareness has no problem holding multiple things in its consciousness. You can be aware of one thing, two things, twenty things, or two million things because awareness is not an arrow. It is a net that you cast. Yes, the objective is to capture something, but the quality of capturing it is completely different. With your mind, you're always shooting it down. "There is an object I want to capture. Let me shoot it." With awareness, you cast the net. It always captures more than what you want to capture, which is perfectly fine. One condition of mindfulness is to watch the breath. No condition says, "Don't watch anything else along with the breath." What if you can watch your whole body perfectly fine? What if you can watch your entire activity in totality? You're driving, and you want to watch your breath, but you are aware of the entire process of driving. So what? Your breath is also included in that.

The key is to know that you don't have to stress about the breath to focus on it. There is a difference between focusing and awareness. Focusing means "I need to only watch my breath." Awareness means "I need to watch my breath." So as long as it continues, this is a beautiful play. It will take some time for you to get it. With a little bit of practice, you will get all these nuances. You'll get all these tricks - "When I'm more relaxed and not too engrossed in the activity, it's easier to watch. Relaxation is the other dimension of consciousness that I have never been able to access. I have only been accessing effort and one-dimensional focus - concentrate, get things done, achieve this, achieve that. I have not been allowing the most important dimension of life, which is the inner being, the consciousness, to observe what's happening so that it can intuitively understand my life."

## BEGIN WITH STUMBLING

It takes practice to be gentle, and as with any practice, when you begin to do something, you will always approach it in its grossest, most outermost way - subtlety comes only with practice. For example, you want to be a dancer. When you begin practicing dance, there is no subtlety. There's no grace there. What are you doing? You're trying to learn the steps. When you're trying to learn the steps, other people don't feel like sitting and watching you learn how to dance. You might say, "Come back after a year. That's when it's enjoyable to watch.

What's happening initially? Everything is crude. There's no subtlety. When you begin to paint, there is no subtlety. There's no sense of scale. There is no sense of intermixing of colors. There's no subtlety of light, of shadow, nothing - because your mind is always gross. The mind is one-dimensional. When you start drawing or painting, notice how the mind paints. It paints like a child. It paints like that because that is how the mind thinks.

If you were to tell the mind to create a house, a coconut tree, and an ocean, notice how it creates them. There would be no connection between that ocean, the coconut tree, and the house. There won't be any merging. Part of the house will not be covered by the coconut tree. Part of the ocean will not be covered by the house because that's not how the mind thinks. The mind is always looking at things independently. "There's the ocean. There's the house, and there's the tree." It's only when we begin to understand that, "I am not painting how things are in nature; I am painting how my mind is seeing it," that we bring in the merging - part of the house is falling on the ocean as a shadow, and part of the ocean is being reflected in the house, and the ocean is not just the ocean. There is a reflection of the house in the ocean. That's when you realize these are not three separate things. They are one thing, but in your mind, they appear to be separate because you have three different words for them.

For the first time, you understand that reality is seamless. There are no houses. There are no trees. There are no oceans. It is just one beautiful tapestry of life. The human mind separates them for convenience and for remembering. It is only focusing on that one thing you want it to focus on because it's using language. Consciousness doesn't use language. Consciousness doesn't recognize the mind. That is why consciousness can hold everything at once, and there is complete flexibility in terms of how much you want to be aware.

I can use my awareness and restrict it to just this house - just this place. I can say, "Just be aware of what's happening inside here. Don't worry about what's happening outside." So any sounds or sensations that are happening inside the house will be picked up, and anything outside is not interesting. Just by giving it such a simple instruction, it can understand "I just need to be aware of this much." But again, remember, it is not focusing on anything in particular. It is still a wide net, but there is a boundary to it. And then you can expand that boundary. It's the same way when you are beginning to watch your breath as a part of your mindfulness practice.

First, you have to start with the smallest possible boundary so that you don't get disturbed, and you develop the ability to watch. The breath is the smallest possible boundary. But still, you're not trying to focus. You're just trying to be aware of your breath. And then slowly, that boundary can be expanded. Now, how is it possible that you can watch your breath and still do something else? It's perfectly possible because you're only aware - you're not focusing.

When you're just aware, notice that awareness is so subtle that it doesn't interfere with the activities of the mind and body. Awareness is always above and beyond the mind and body. It's almost like there is a third entity that is sitting above your regular cognition and watching everything that is happening. But unless you learn the art of watching through that third entity, you are only dealing with the mind and the body, and that's where the limitation comes in. When you are moving between the limitations of the mind and body, you can only juggle between focusing on this or that. But when you move higher in another sense, when you move deeper in relaxation, you can be aware of multiple things without any problem.

That is why for the first three weeks or so, mindfulness is hard. It is hard because the quality of what you're trying to do is alien to the mind. The mind is not used to this concept. The mind only knows how to focus. With enough practice, you will understand the nuances of awareness, the subtlety of awareness, and the dance of awareness. That's when you will ask, "How have I been missing this? I've been looking at the world through a small keyhole when the whole roof is open. There is nothing there. All I had to do was just climb up and I could have seen the whole world. I could have seen the green and the blue. I could have seen the clouds moving in the sky. I could have seen the phenomenon of life unfolding. I've missed all that because I've been looking through the keyhole of my tiny window."

It has all been guesswork. Our whole life has been a guesswork. We don't know who we are and we don't know where we are going because we are looking through the keyhole of the mind. Mindfulness brings out that creature that has a million eyes, not just two. Its cognition is limitless. Its ability to see is expansive. It is pure light, pure awareness, pure aliveness, and you cannot even fathom the beauty of that thing. That's when you will realize, "This is what I've been searching for - the peace, the happiness, the relaxation, the bliss - I've been searching through the mind. I've been searching through the activities of the mind. I've been searching through the concepts that I created using the keyhole of the mind. All the while, what I needed was a way to step away from the mind and dive into the deeper realms of life. It's like somebody gave me a mango but nobody told me that it's edible. I've been looking at it. I've been smelling it. Once in a while, I probably even licked the skin. I didn't know that the mango tastes this good."

That's what we've been doing with life. We've been praying to it. Sometimes we've been worshiping it. We've been keeping it in our closet; we take it out, admire it, and show it to our friends. The only thing that we have not done is sink our teeth into that juicy pulp. That's life. Then we don't need philosophy. We don't need theories. Once we know that life is complete at this very moment, we don't have to go anywhere. We don't have to move into the future. We don't have to do great things in life. We are the kings of our own kingdom. We are born with all that we are searching for, with just a small difference - the direction in which we are looking. Our direction has become outward. We have forgotten the inside. That's what mindfulness is - it is just a reminder that there is an inner you, and it is deep, vast, juicy, succulent, and nourishing. The outside is only images.

## GETTING PAST THE IMAGES

How long can you be satisfied with images? Sooner or later, you will realize it is not nourishing you. Isn't this the same thing that's happening in the world? We pursue our desires. "Okay. Let me build this house, then I'm going to be the happiest person in the world." What happens the moment you finish it? At the very moment, its beauty begins to diminish. You will enjoy it for a while, then you get used to it. Something that you worked on for years, and after that, it just moved into the background.

Then you pursue another desire, and another and another. The world is a cancerous growth of desires. There is no meaning, no purpose; everybody is running, everybody is chasing. And why are we so disturbed? Because we are trying to find satisfaction in images - self-image, not in the self. How can self-image satisfy us? Let me give you a photograph of a mango. Be satisfied with it. Yes. You can frame it. You can admire it for a while. But your desire to taste it can never be fulfilled. Your desire to eat that mango will always be there. That's what life is. Life has depth. And we have only been skimming the surface. Watching the breath is just a reminder. It is just a prop. It is just a method to come to the present moment. It is just a method to tell ourselves, "Enough of this outward. Come inward. Yes, it's going to be challenging because my mind is so used to looking on the outside. It tries to turn watching the breath into an outside activity. It starts talking about it. Oh, watching the breath - it's so easy - watch the breath, watch the breath."

Don't talk about it. Watch the breath. The mind doesn't care about the actual activity. It wants to talk about it. That's it. Sometimes it sings about it. And then it keeps on qualifying it. "Do it like this. Do it like that." Even when you're doing it right, the mind cannot shut up. More often than not, you are aware, but you cannot keep your mind quiet. And that's where the problem is. Your mind tells you that this is not awareness - how can it be so simple? How can it be this simple? Awareness is so simple, so subtle, and so beautiful, but it's the most difficult thing because the mind does not get it.

## SWEEP THE FLOOR

A student goes to the Zen master and asks him to teach him how to be mindful. The master tells him to sweep the floor. The student tells the master, "I want to learn mindfulness." "Sweep the floor." So the student says, "Okay. I'll sweep the floor." So he sweeps the floor for quite a while, and he comes back. "Master, I've swept the floor. It's completely clean. Now teach me mindfulness." The master again says to sweep the floor. And the student gets frustrated after a while. "What is this? I've been asking you to teach me mindfulness. I want to learn how to be mindful. You're just wanting me to clean your house. I'm not going to do it. I want to learn mindfulness."

Then the master says, "Clean the house, but while cleaning the house, watch the one who's cleaning the house. Be mindful of the person cleaning the house. Be mindful of the one sweeping." And then the student asks, "Is that mindfulness?" The master replies, "Yes, that is mindfulness." "That's it? That should be easy. All I have to do is watch myself sweep the floor. That's it. That is mindfulness."

Then the student asks, "Why is it difficult? What is so great about it? It's so easy, I can do it." The master says, "Sweeping the floor is not difficult. Watching yourself sweep the floor is not difficult. But remembering to do this is difficult. That is the whole challenge. The practice is not hard. It is just remembering to watch that is hard."

When we don't remember, it's just the mind. It just forgets. When you remember it, it is the easiest. It is the simplest of tasks to complete. Watch everything - watch the breath, watch the body, watch your movement, watch the sensations on your skin. With a little bit of practice, you will know the qualitative difference between being in the present moment and being lost in thought. You will know the difference as clearly as day and night. When you are aware, there's a lightness to your activities. There is a sense of certainty about what you're doing. It's almost like bright lights flood your activity, and you can clearly see what's happening.

On the contrary, imagine that time when you were angry or frustrated about something - someone made you angry. What happened? Your awareness was lost. It felt like you were thrown into a dark room. Anger just feels like being in a dark room. There are so many things happening, but you don't know how to look at them. You don't know what's happening. You don't know which thought to hold on to. That is the difference. When you are aware, it's not complicated - it's not difficult. When you're not aware, that is when you will know how much of a difference being aware and not being aware makes.

When you're not being mindful, that's when you know that you are in a dark room and you're trying to look for answers. But when you're aware, answers come to you because you are closest to aliveness, the very medium through which everything is being transferred. Because you're closest to the medium, closest to the seat of what's happening, with a little bit of patience, the answers will come flooding in. When you're not aware because you're so far away from the present moment, you have to run behind answers - that is the world. Look at the world. Look at people. They wake up in the morning and begin running. Where are they running? What are they running towards? A future that never comes? A tomorrow that is imaginary? That is humanity. That is the direction in which we are going.

We are complaining that there's no peace, there's no relaxation, no contentment or joy. Why? Because the inner is forgotten. Initially, it's a challenge because your mind confuses awareness with focus. Keep dancing. Keep falling. Keep learning the steps. Keep painting the house, the ocean, and the tree separately. Slowly, they'll merge. Slowly, you'll become a better painter. Slowly, you'll become a better dancer. Slowly, you'll become a better meditator. And slowly, you will become better at being aware. Then a day will come when you will be surrounded by a thick fog of aliveness. Wherever you go, it will be there. You can't escape it, because once you go that deep and connect to it you don't have to make an effort to be aware - it's right there. You just know how to connect with it. Until that happens, it's a little bit of a challenge, but not impossible.

Where the Hell are You Going?

# CHAPTER FIVE

# SLOW DOWN

There are many different ways in which you can approach mindfulness, but the ultimate objective is to break the regular pattern of the mind. That is the objective of mindfulness as a technique. Of course, the reason you're doing it has a bigger purpose - there is a grander purpose. Just behind the veil of thoughts hides everything you're looking for. Your thought process is so continuous, so thick, and so real that you see nothing beyond it. Your life is governed by your thoughts. The boundary of your being is your thoughts, so if a thought tells you this is who you are, you have to accept it. There's no arguing with it because you don't know there is something beyond the thoughts.

## BREAKING THE CHAIN OF THOUGHTS

The purpose of any mindfulness technique is to first observe this thought process that is happening all the time - without any break - and see if you can stop it. Although it may seem like an impossible task, "How do I stop a chain of thoughts? How do I interfere with my thought process? It is my thought process. I am thinking, so I'm deeply invested in it. If I had no interest in thinking about something, why would I think about it?" The problem or difficulty in trying to be mindful is that, in a way, you have to contradict yourself. You have to contradict your desires. You have to contradict your thought process, and that can only happen when you develop a sense of skepticism toward your thoughts - not blindly accept and trust everything you're seeing. At that moment, your mind will try to convince you, "This is very important. This thought process will either make or break you." In reality, it could just be humming a song, but the mind takes it so seriously that it wants you to engage with it. It wants you to listen to that song. Although you can give it a simple instruction, "Not now - I want to be quiet," the mind will not listen.

The mind only understands how to grab your attention and continue to do whatever it is engaged in at that moment. It wants to just be in that mechanical routine. It has a certain rhythm, a certain pace of doing things, and a certain pattern of doing things. More than anything else, the mind is a pattern. The content might change, but if you closely observe the mind, the pace at which it moves in different situations, the way it moves, and the rhythm at which it moves are directly connected to your emotions.

When you're angry or frustrated, your thoughts move fast. Anger is a response that happens when your mind is moving fast. If your mind is moving slowly, you can have angry thoughts, but they will never come out as anger. The entire quality of that anger would be different, but the thought process is the same. What has changed? The pace has changed. You can use this quality of the mind to trick the mind into altering its state. You can use a mindfulness technique of slowing down and sometimes even stopping for no reason, just for the sake of slowing down or stopping. If you're able to do it, your mind gets confused. The pattern is broken. In fact, in psychological terms, it is called pattern interrupt. Psychologists use it all the time.

What is the definition of madness? What is the definition of insanity? You're stuck in a loop that you're unable to get out of. That's what madness is. If you're able to step out of it at will, and if you're able to get in and out of the loop, that is called life. Madness is when you have no control over how long you want to be stuck in that loop, and how deep you want to go. The mind is always in some state of madness, even when it appears to be perfectly sane. Even when it seems to be in its most lucid state, there is an underlying madness in the mind because there is unconsciousness in the depths of the mind.

## THE NATURE OF THE MIND

A thought process has started, and mechanically, the mind is following through on that thought process. This happens not only when you are deeply engaged in your thoughts - it happens all the time. The mind never stops when it actually should. Unless you make a conscious effort to stop it, it just keeps on going.

You think about something - you want to accomplish something. The instruction is given, and then you start acting. Once the action is complete, the mind should stop. But more often than not, it doesn't. It just continues in the same pattern because the mind is moving. The mind is momentum. The unconscious is the energy that drives the mind, so the mind will not understand the language of slowing down. It will just add your words to its vocabulary: "Slow down." That's it. It will just add it to another phrase. "Slow down. Okay. Stop. So what?" If you tell the mind to stop after a while, it will repeat the sentence, then stop, and then continue the sentence.

That's the nature of the mind. The mind does not understand "stop" literally. What is the meaning of "stop?" In the mind, everything is a thought. Even "stopping" and "slowing down" are thoughts. This is what happens when we are angry, frustrated, stressed, and disturbed. We try to have a conversation with the mind. We try to control it by diverting its attention, by giving it different instructions, but because it is in that momentum, because it is in that loop, whatever we add to it turns it into the same emotion. That's why instructing the mind does not matter. What are the contents of your thoughts when you are angry? Whatever you add to that moment becomes anger. When you are sad or depressed, positive thoughts don't mean anything. That is why all this philosophizing about thinking positively doesn't always work, because when the mind is in a certain emotional loop, it takes anything and everything available and turns it into that emotion.

This is where we fail to understand the real nature of the mind. The mind is not just a collection of thoughts. It is a collection of emotions. It has its own momentum, movement, and pattern. So instead of trying to have a conversation with the mind, you can use a technique to abruptly stop it. One way to do it is to - for no reason - try to slow down your thought patterns. Make a conscious effort to think slowly. You don't have to change what you're thinking. You don't have to alter your thought process, because you're deeply invested in those thoughts and don't want to let go of them. That is the challenge. Right? If I were to tell you, "Just stop thinking." What is the difficulty? Just stop thinking. Well, the difficulty is that these thoughts are deeply connected to what you're doing at the moment, what you want to be doing, and they're already in a set pattern.

That's where you cannot simply instruct your mind or your thoughts to stop. It's not going to stop - but you can slow it down. Yes, continue to think. You have to trick the mind into believing that you are allowing it to do what it wants to do so that it doesn't completely reject your new method. But at the same time, you are artfully dealing with the mind. Even without awareness of the mind, you are slowly taking away its power. You're slowly taking away its control because the mind doesn't know what you know. It doesn't know that it is just a blind pattern. The mind thinks that it is fully autonomous, that it can think, judge, and all that. This is all fine, but the mind does not understand that by slowing it down over some time, you can regain control. When you try to slow it down, it won't resist very much as opposed to trying to change the thought process or suddenly stopping it.

Slowing down has always worked. That's why it's one of the most important mindfulness techniques. If you were to walk into a spiritual community, what is the first thing you notice when you watch the students or the seekers moving about? The first thing you notice is that they're not in a hurry. If you see them in a hurry moving from one place to another, then get out of that place. They have failed to understand the most important aspect of mindfulness, which is slowing down. If they are truly practicing mindfulness you will notice that there is a deliberate, conscious movement in their actions. Their bodies are not flopping around. They are not moving unconsciously. The pace has slowed down. You can recognize that there is something else going on with their minds and bodies. It is not just a mechanical process; there is a conscious, deliberate effort to slow down.

Slowing down is an ancient practice. Monasteries and spiritual schools have used it because they understood very clearly that if you can slow down the mind, you are allowing yourself to control it. It is hardest to control the mind when it is moving the fastest - when it is jumping from one thought to another without any break. This happens when you're stressed, angry, or worried about something. Those are the moments when it is hard to control your thoughts.

In a way, you can use slowing down as a form of reverse psychology to tell the mind to continue to do what it wants to do, but at a slower pace. Deliberately slow down your actions. If you're walking, make a conscious decision to slow down. And what is the hurry? This whole idea that if you don't hurry, you will never be able to get something done has to be overcome. You have to go beyond that. You should know that even if you do things at half speed, you can still accomplish all that you are trying to accomplish. You can accomplish it better because you're not hurrying and making a lot of mistakes. Even simple activities that you do daily - if you slow down - might take a little longer to finish, but because you're doing it consciously, you're avoiding all the unnecessary mistakes. Even if you were to look at it from a purely practical standpoint, it makes sense to slow down.

More importantly, by slowing down, you are introducing autonomy. You are introducing consciousness. You're introducing yourself to the thought process. So next time, when there is a thought process that you want to control - because it is moving slower - it becomes that much easier. Again, the objective of mindfulness is not to control the thoughts, but if you can slow them down, you can watch them more clearly. Start with simple activities that you do daily, and remind yourself to slow down. Know that every time your mind refuses to slow down, it wants to hurry. It's trying to tell you, "I want to remain insane," because slowing down is sanity for the mind. Things are becoming clearer. You're able to listen to your inner voice more clearly. You're able to observe your thoughts more clearly. You're able to understand your emotions better, and your mind doesn't like any of this. The mind wants to remain in darkness. That is its power. So every time you try to hurry, just slow down for no reason. Your mind will ask for an explanation. "Why? What is the purpose of slowing down? What is the necessity of slowing down?" Listen to this, but don't try to argue with the mind. Don't try to give reasons. Don't try to give justifications as to why it should slow down, because that is what it wants you to do. It wants you to get into another argument.

Instead, listen to the same conversation but at a slower pace. Insist on the mind narrating the same thing at a slower pace. Initially, it might say, "Why are you slowing down? What is the purpose of slowing down? What is the necessity of slowing down?" Then you say the same thing slowly. Then the mind asks, "What is the necessity of slowing down? What is the purpose of slowing down?" Now, what's happening there? The content is the same. The thought process is the same. For the first time, you can control the mind because it is listening to you. If you are successful at instructing the mind to "slow down," with a little bit of practice, eventually your mind will understand and start talking to you slowly. Half of your problems, your mental blocks, unnecessary anger, and worry disappear right there. Why? Because you can have a conversation now.

Before, there was no conversation with the mind. The mind was yelling from the rooftops, and whatever you could hear - a little bit here and there - you were trying to make sense of what it was trying to say. By the time you fully understood what it was trying to say, it had gone on to the next thought process, then the next, and the next. It wasn't allowing you to see the conflict.


## BRIDGING THE MIND AND BODY

At the end of the day, what is a thought? It is a conflict. It is trying to resolve something - otherwise, there is no need to think. Thinking by itself is an incomplete process. You're thinking because something is undone, you want to do it, and your thoughts are reminding you to do it. But what happens when this reminder is happening at such a pace that you have to catch up with the mind to understand what it's trying to say? This is the birthplace of all kinds of disturbances - when we are playing catch-up with the mind.

A simple technique: Slow down. Slow down your breathing. Slow down your body movements. Slow down the way you turn. Slow down the way you react to situations. The content is the same. When you want to get angry, get angry, but get angry slowly. If you want to shout at someone, shout. No problem. But do it slowly. You don't even have to change the volume. You only have to slow the pace. Notice how magically, just slowing down changes the whole internal landscape. Suddenly, there is more space for you to move around. There is more space, more emptiness for you to endure in your thoughts - just a simple method. And then, once in a while, if you can succeed in slowing down, just stop.

You're taking a walk, in your regular state of mind, and you're not even thinking about it - you're not aware of it. Your mind is somewhere else. There is a disconnect between your body and your mind. That disconnect is what we are trying to bridge. Mindfulness is about bringing your mind, body, and your self into alignment so that you can consciously observe what's happening. As of now, conscious observation is not happening because your body is doing one thing and your mind is doing something else. Your mind is not interested in what the body is doing; it thinks it's far superior. It believes that watching the body move is a waste of time - meanwhile, it could be arguing with someone. It could be planning something that needs to be done tomorrow, or worrying about yesterday. That is what the mind is. That's what the mind wants to do. There's a beautiful Zen saying: "They say it doesn't matter whether you're moving up or down the ladder. As long as you're on the ladder, it's still wobbly. You have to get down on the ground to experience your true nature."

The mind is an entity that is constantly moving up and down the ladder between the past and the future. It doesn't see the ground. It is obsessed with the ladder. It wants to hold on to it, and it is stuck in that groove. It is perfectly okay for the mind to take a break once in a while, but it does not even understand the concept of taking a break. It doesn't believe in such ideas - "What do you mean by taking a break? Are you telling me to just stop thinking? How do I do that?"

Mind is mind. When there are no thoughts, there is no mind. You're telling the mind to disappear, and it does not understand disappearing because you are giving it instructions through words and ideas. The problem with trying to come back to the present moment has more to do with the way we communicate with the mind than anything else. We are so used to communicating with the mind in its language, that when we tell it to get down from that ladder and stay on the ground for a while, it doesn't understand. So communication has to come from a different dimension. It cannot come from thoughts.

## MINDFULNESS STARTS IN THE BODY

Any mindfulness technique you practice cannot be a direction that you give using words and ideas. It has to be something that starts in the body. Your body has to give it instructions. If you want to slow down, you don't have to tell your mind to slow down. The moment you do that, you are involving yourself in the conversation with your mind - and it's the same thing. The mind will slow down and turn that into a different idea - instead, pattern interrupt. Suddenly slow down for no reason. The moment you remember that "I can slow down," it does not matter what it is that you're doing. In most activities, you can slow down without hurting yourself or others.

Of course, you don't want to just arbitrarily slow down while, let's say, driving in traffic - that could cause an accident. Most of the time, slowing down - if there are people around you - will just look a little odd. Other than that, slowing down has no negative impact. If you suddenly start slowing down, if you start walking or smiling slowly, if you start talking slowly, people might think you've gone mad because they're used to a certain you, they're used to a certain pattern. But that is a small sacrifice you can make to regain your sanity and regain control of your mind.

Look at your life as a pattern that is deeply set. You're not doing most of the things. Most things are simply happening. You're not consciously choosing to breathe. You're not consciously choosing to turn or sit, to shift your weight here and there, yet most of these things are happening. At the most, you're only acknowledging them.

The objective, or purpose, of mindfulness is to do these things, not to let them simply happen. It's to say, "I want to make life happen. I want to do my walking. I want to do my moving. I want to be the one in control of these activities, not the other way around." It is a small shift in quality, but it makes a huge difference. The control shifts from the automatic mind to the conscious being. You will know the value of this in moments of frustration and anger; you cannot even jump into unconscious anger once you start practicing this enough. Once you learn the art of slowing down, you can apply it in all dimensions. You can apply it to your physical movements, your mental patterns, and the way you look at a problem. Just slow down and once in a while, completely break the pattern and just stop.

You're taking a walk. The moment you remember that you can slow down, slow down. And for no reason, just stop. It doesn't matter. If there are a few people around you, they might look at you but that doesn't matter. You are telling the mind, "I will decide." Because what the mind is used to is giving an instruction and forgetting all about it. The mind wants to give you instructions and disappear. It wants you to walk, and then it wants to go somewhere else and be in an alternate universe.

## DON'T ARGUE WITH THE MIND

We are using mindfulness to tell the mind that there are not two universes - there are not two worlds. As of now, the world of our body and the world of our mind are divided - there's a huge separation between the two. When you start practicing mindfulness, that is when you will see how big a separation this is. That is the foundation of all the chaos and confusion - we are constantly running between the mind and the body, trying to get them to communicate with each other. Otherwise, you can simply tell the mind what to do and what it should not do. There should be no difficulty whatsoever in conversing with the mind. If you're taking a walk and want to slow down, you should be able to slow down. If you want to stop, you should stop. If you want to turn around and come back, you should be able to do it. You're sitting, you're eating, and you're fully conscious of your eating. Once you know that your stomach is full, it does not matter how much food is on the plate; you should be able to tell the body, "That's enough," and your mind should say, "Yes, that's enough."

On the contrary, look what's happening. For everything you want to do, you have to win the argument with your mind - even the simplest of things. All your energy is being drained by this because your mind isn't paying attention. So you become conscious. You know that the mind does not understand that this much food is enough. The body is already full, but the mind doesn't care; it's stuffing the food in, and you're giving the instruction, "No, that's enough." But there is such a big separation between the body and the mind that you have to travel back and forth between them. You have to take the language of the body and decode it for the mind, and you have to take the language of the mind and decode it for the body. It's an exhaustive process that is happening all the time.

Even the simplest of instructions that we are trying to give to the mind and the body require this much effort. That is what mindfulness changes. The only effort mindfulness asks of you is to put in the effort to bridge this gap. Once the gap is bridged, all the other efforts disappear. That is why, when you initially begin practicing mindfulness, it seems like an uphill battle. It seems like a great challenge. Why? We've been living in two different universes with two completely different entities, trying to get them to work together. If they're able to listen to each other, that is harmony. That is coherence. That is in alignment with life.

Why is it that animals, irrespective of their deep unconsciousness, complete their actions in the moment? They don't sit and argue with their mind. A dog could be sleeping, and when it hears a sound, if it wants to bark, it does not sit and argue with the mind. "Should I bark now? What's going to happen if I bark?" Nothing. It just jumps up and barks. This is a spontaneous response. Why? Because the mind is not too far away from the body. Look at all the creatures in existence. You'll be amazed at how quickly an animal can spring into action. For example, look at a heron, or a crane. It could be standing in the water, absolutely still, waiting for a fish. It could stand still for hours without flinching or moving. But when it wants to, when it sees the fish, there's hardly any gap between that intent, that decision to catch the fish, and the action. It happens instantaneously. Why? Because the mind was not walking on a beach somewhere.

The problem with us is that when we try to do something like that, when the fish comes in, our mind is somewhere else. It is doing something else. We are absent-minded. That's the definition of being absent-minded, which means the mind is not with the body. By the time we decide, the fish will be gone. That is why we are pathetic hunters. When we are left in nature all alone, we are so clumsy - not because our bodies don't have the abilities. Not because our minds don't have the abilities. We are as capable as any other creature in existence, but we have gotten into the habit of living in two different worlds.

## THE OBSESSION OF THINKING

We have become so obsessed with thinking that we regard all the activities of the body - most of the activities that the body performs - as a useless waste of time. "I want to be thinking about something. I want to be doing something else." This is the beginning of all neuroses - where the mind does not want to be near the body. What happens when you slow down? When you slow down, you have to bring the mind closer to the body, because who is giving the conscious instruction for the body to slow down? If your mind is drifting somewhere and if you have completely forgotten your body, then nobody is controlling the pace of the movement. It is all happening autonomously. When you deliberately slow down, invariably, you're bringing the mind from drifting to the present moment. You're doing it again and again. As long as you are consciously slowing your movements, your mind has to be there watching that movement. Why? Because it is new. The mind will leave the body and drift only when it is sure what the body is doing, has a set pattern, and is in a safe environment.

When you slow the body down, the mind panics. "Oh, something different is happening here. It is not a regular walk. I can go to the beach later. Let me see what's happening with the body." Because the first responsibility of the mind is to safeguard the body, when you put the body in a new environment, the mind is alert. It is only in the regular pattern that the mind drifts. When you go to a new place or hear a new sound, your mind comes racing back. It does not matter where it is - it comes back immediately. But if it's the same thing the body is doing - same brushing the teeth, walking, cleaning, cooking - the mind says, "I'm gone." Total disconnect.

We are literally, physically disconnected from our true nature. The body is in one dimension and the mind is in another. A simple method of slowing down brings them together. You're telling the mind, "It doesn't matter. Watch the body." It could be simple breathing. "Just watch it." It could be simple walking. "Just watch it. It's fine. You don't have to accomplish anything. I permit you to waste your time. I permit you to not accomplish anything great." Just be with the body and once in a while, completely stop. You're eating - slow down, and for no reason, just stop. Just watch your biochemistry. Just watch what's happening when you stop. Watch where the mind is when you stop. You might be eating while watching television. You're neither conscious of what you're eating nor of what you're watching on television, your mind is drifting somewhere. It's just picked up those images and gone somewhere. But for whatever reason, suddenly, if you stop, your mind comes back and says, "What happened? Everything was fine. We were all perfectly happy in our unconsciousness. Why did you stop?" That is what you want the mind to do. You want the mind to observe consciousness.

## OBSERVING ACTION

To observe action is to observe the body - so much so that a day should come when the mind refuses to go anywhere away from the body. It should not even move an inch away from the body. That is when you will become fully centered in your being. Then there is no dichotomy. There is no conflict. There is no fear. There is no stress or anxiety. Because you are, your body is, your mind is, and they're all in this moment. And how easy is it to control them? They're all right here. The mind does not want to drift. It has stopped drifting.

That's when you realize that this drifting business of the mind, although it seemed important, was simply a pattern of no use whatsoever. That was the pattern that was creating all kinds of unnecessary chaos and confusion. A simple method is to slow down your actions, slow down your thought patterns, slow down your response to things, and just turn everything down a little bit. Life's going to be more meaningful. It's going to be deeper. Initially, you will feel like the world is in a hurry and everyone else is accomplishing so many things. What am I doing? But very quickly, you will understand the value of slowing down. When you're not constantly arguing with the mind, you can give instructions to the mind and the body in the present moment, and they simply follow. There is no greater joy than that. When you want to sit, you should be able to do so without any argument in your mind. That is happiness. That is bliss.

We keep searching for grand things, but in actuality, whatever we are searching for is the simplest of things. Can I smile when I want to? Can I cry when I want to? Can I sleep when I want to? Can I wake up when I want to? Can I do what I want to do? That's it. That is freedom. That is happiness. It's not about all the different things you can do. It is about - can you do one thing? The question is very profound. Ask yourself this question: Can I walk? You will be surprised by the answer. The question is not, "Can I walk efficiently? Can I walk fast?" No. Do you even know how to walk? Just because the body is walking doesn't mean that you are walking. The only time you can tell with absolute certainty that you are walking is when your body is walking, your mind is watching that walking, and you are watching the mind watching the walking. All three are aligned. Your whole universe changed in that moment. That is when you can say with absolute certainty, "Yes, I can walk." Until then, you can at most say, "Well, I think my body can walk. I think my body can eat. I think my body can sleep. I don't know if I can do any of these things because I keep drifting. I don't consciously eat with my body. I don't consciously move with my body, so there's a disconnect." The day you're able to say with absolute certainty that you can consciously choose to do something and do it, that's when you know mindfulness has worked. Slowing down has worked, and stopping has worked.

## CHAPTER SIX

## LOST IN DOING

*How can I be mindful while doing other activities?*

Mindfulness is necessary because we so easily get lost in activities. Activities are not just what you do physically. The bigger activity that is going on continuously and that you pay very little attention to, is the mental activity. Physical activity is just a small part of mental activity. In the endless continuum of mental activity, once in a while, something springs out and becomes a physical activity. To know how crazy and idiotic the mind is, you only have to visualize doing everything your mind is thinking. Even for a single moment, if you were to entertain that thought, you would see that would be the definition of madness.

If you were to act on every thought, every impulse, every desire, and every sensation, your actions would be very close to the actions of a total madman. So what is it that separates you from a lunatic? What is it that separates your actions from the actions of a madman? The only thing that separates you is your conscious intervention. You consciously intervene between your mind and body. You don't let the body do whatever the mind wants to do, because you know that is just madness. Now, what is this conscious interference doing? Who is consciously interfering? Your mind is crazy. Your body is a perfect servant, doing whatever the mind tells it to do. The mind has total autonomy. It listens to no one. The body has zero autonomy. It has no direction of its own. It simply follows the instructions of the mind. Between these two, there has to be a third entity that is coordinating the actions and observing the mind as well as the body - "This can be done. This cannot be done. This should be done. This should not be done. I want to do this. I don't want to do this." This has to be someone very conscious, very intelligent, someone who's fully aware of what you need as a being - someone who's fully aware of the necessity for your well-being, the necessity for your safety and security.

## CONSCIOUS INTERVENTION

There is someone who's consciously intervening. There is something - there is no denying it. How do we know this? Throughout the day, when we are going about our different activities, there come moments when we pause and reevaluate an action. We check. That check, that pause, that stop - that conscious moment - is mindfulness. That intervening force is mindfulness. Once you understand this, then the next step is to ask, "How do I exercise this choice more often throughout the day? How do I intervene more? How do I assert my stance and say, You're passing through my space?" Your space is the present moment. The mind is simply the past - it knows nothing of the present moment. But the body is in the present moment. The actions of the body are in the present moment. The mind can imagine whatever it wants, but if it has to push the body into action, even for a single moment, it has to pass through the present.

That is where you are as a gatekeeper, and you're looking at the mind, deciding how the action is going to be performed - or if it's even necessary. So the real challenge in mindfulness is identifying action before it happens. Once the action happens, you have missed it. Once the thought passes through the present moment, it passes through your guard. For whatever reason, if you were asleep at that moment, the mind gave instructions to the body, and the body started following them.

Now the task of becoming mindful of what you are doing is doubly difficult because the body is already in the process of acting. Something has to stop that action. Now it requires additional effort. More often than not, you cannot even remember to stop. You just continue. As the action finishes, as the action is coming to an end, that is when you become aware, become mindful. If you didn't want to do that or if you hadn't been mindful, that is when you realize, "Oh, I missed it. I wanted to be mindful over the last thirty minutes and I haven't." So the challenge of mindfulness is really how to identify action before it happens. Now here is the trick - the most important thing, and if you can get this you will get mindfulness. You don't have to complicate it any more than this.

You're there at the gate, watching what the mind and the body are doing. If you get a little too curious and try to go into the mind to see what it is doing, you will get trapped. The mind is so smart that it can completely hijack you. That is one way in which you miss being mindful - you go into your thoughts. You transform the action of mindfulness, which is about being in the present moment, into contemplation of mindfulness, thinking about mindfulness, and all that the mind enjoys. The moment you start approaching mindfulness using your mind or you try to control your actions using your mind, you are trapped.

What happens if mindfulness does begin with the mind? You start dreaming. Mindfulness that begins with the mind is nothing but a dream. For example, in your dream, while you're asleep, you are still aware of certain things. You are aware of your fears, and you are aware of your desires - you're aware of a lot of things. But because you are in the mind, you are just a part of the dreaming process. Even though awareness is part of the dreaming process, remember, the mind is so smart, intelligent, and cunning that it can even replicate the perception of self-awareness. It can make you feel like you're being self-aware while completely trapping you in the dream. It doesn't even care whether it's real or not. Because you've been asking for self-awareness, it will manufacture it for you. If you're asking for mindfulness, it will manufacture it for you. It will create an environment, a scenario that appears like mindfulness, and then it will try to convince you that whatever you've been doing is mindfulness.

Your dreaming process isn't mindfulness, so you cannot start with the mind. There is only one other place to start. Start from the body and start where the body is in inaction, not in action. Look for that moment when the body is not doing anything. That is when you become mindful. That point is the only point at which you can be mindful. You cannot be mindful of the mind. You cannot be mindful of an action after it has already started, because that's like trying to stop a freight train. It is much harder. You can stop it though, after enough practice, after you've spent enough time in mindfulness, and after you've understood what mindfulness is. After your practice has strengthened itself, you can stop not just the actions of the body, you can even stop the actions of the mind. You can have so much control over guarding that gate, that even for a moment, if you miss a thought and it escapes you, you can go and find it. If an action misses you, you can stop it in the middle. You could be running at breakneck speed, and somewhere in the middle, you can become fully aware of that running because your practice has kicked in. But initially, when you're beginning your mindfulness practice, there's no other place to start than with the body, when the body is not performing any action. You have to start with something very simple.

It is the trick of the mind to test your mindfulness. It will push you to test your mindfulness in the most difficult of situations - it wants you to fail. And when you're unable to be mindful, it will say, "Come, join my party. What are you trying to do fighting against me and the body? We've been doing our thing without your interference. Who are you to interfere now? I've done it like this for your entire life. I've kept you alive. I've kept you safe. What more do you want?" Your response would be: "You also put me in so much chaos. You've taken away my peace of mind. You've taken away my relaxation. You have occupied my whole house, and you've given me one small corner.

And even there, I need your permission to be in the present moment. No. No. I want to clean up my house. Yes. You are useful, but I'm going to give you your place." You will tell the body, "Yes. You're useful, but you have your place." That clearing-out process is what mindfulness is.

Start with a moment of inaction. It happens at the moment of decision when you're about to do something new. Let's say you decide to take a walk. At that very moment, you know that the mind is giving instructions to the body, and you're about to take a walk. That is when you can become fully aware of yourself and start watching the action. "Let me watch this walk." Like this, you can watch any activity. As long as you are aware, at that moment when the activity is beginning, you can watch your walking, your talking, your eating, and all your simple daily activities without any problem.

## BECOMING AWARE OF ACTIONS

Now, it's important to understand that there are various levels of activity, in terms of how much they draw our attention. Roughly, we can categorize them into three different types of activities. The first type is activities that don't consume too much of our attention, and that do not require too much interference. These are simple daily routine activities such as walking, talking, brushing the teeth, and eating.

The next set of activities requires a little bit of skill, and a little bit of accumulated knowledge, but is still very close to where the body is - gardening, knitting, sewing, painting, drawing - most of the creative things we do. All those can be categorized as activities that require medium interference and induce medium levels of stress. You're not overly stressed when you're painting, drawing, or gardening, but there's a little bit more stress involved when compared to brushing your teeth or eating. But you can see how, compared to the stress levels when you're eating, the stress level is slightly higher when you're doing any of these other activities.

Then there are the activities that are highly stressful because they don't involve the body. Anything where the body is not required, when the activity has become purely mental, the stress level of that activity would be very high. Without the body to interfere, the mind can go on thinking about it. The mind can go on creating its imagination. That is what leads to that stressful, chaotic space.

You have to start with the simplest of activities. - activities where your mind is not necessary - there's no need to be thinking. For example, when you're brushing your teeth, what is the necessity to be thinking? There is no need to think at all. While you're eating, why is it necessary to be thinking? There's no necessity, but the mind is constantly thinking. Now that's what you're trying to address. That is what you're trying to control. In this constant flow of thoughts, you want a gap - you want space. You can start with activities that are watchable: while taking a bath, while taking a walk, or while simply sitting and relaxing just before going to bed. You can find innumerable activities that are not stressful where mindfulness can be applied. Then you can slowly move to slightly stressful activities that require a little bit of skill and a little bit of additional effort, which encompasses about eighty to ninety percent of your daily activities. Most of us are not doing highly stressful activities. Even when we are doing a highly stressful job, it is stressful only in certain moments.

With enough practice, you can become perfectly aware. You can become fully aware of all your actions, and once you reach that point where the majority of your activities are watched, where is the stress? Where is the disturbance? Where is the unnecessary fear? Where is the unnecessary anger? Because everything is passing through the present moment and you are there, watching every activity, that is how mindfulness becomes a long-term, continuous, systematic practice that you can incorporate into your life by knowing that it starts with simple activities.

Mindfulness is challenging to incorporate into daily activities because, more often than not, we are thinking about being mindful when we are not. When we are stressed, anxious, disturbed, or already halfway down the path of doing something, that's when we remember, "Oh, I missed being mindful." And because we missed it, we try to force it, and if we are unable to be mindful, then it creates its cycle of negativity - "Oh, I'm trying. I'm failing, I'm trying, and I'm failing." That is why it is important to start with the watchable activities. You can even make a simple list of all the watchable activities that don't require any level of skill and don't require your mind. You will not hurt yourself by brushing your teeth if you are not watchful. Those are the activities - activities that don't matter whether you watch or don't watch. Those are the activities to which you can bring watchfulness and mindfulness, and then you can watch those activities that require your attention and the influence of your mind, and ultimately, those activities where your mind is completely engulfed. In those moments, you need mindfulness the most.

Mindfulness is all about watching the body - not the mind. It is watching the body right from the moment it is beginning to perform an action. If you missed it, it's fine. Start again before it picks up the next activity. That is how you keep coming back again and again. Eventually, the practice will deepen, and you can be present in everything you do.

Where the Hell are You Going?

## CHAPTER SEVEN

## THE OBSTACLE COURSE

There are a few important things to understand in terms of what the main obstacles are to mindfulness. You can have the right technique - you could be given the most perfect technique, but if there is an inner conflict in terms of what the technique is making you do and your self-image, you would not be able to stick with it for too long. Because anything you stick to for a long time will eventually become a part of your being, it has to align with your self-image. It has to align with who you are as a person and your understanding of life. If there is a conflict there, then the technique is of no use.

This is a fundamental mistake most people make while picking up a technique or a method. They pick a technique that sounds nice, or they pick a popular technique - let's say, Buddhist meditation. We don't even inquire if it is the right kind of meditation for us. Because we want to follow in the footsteps of the Buddha, we simply borrow the technique. But somewhere, if it does not align with who you are as a person, sooner or later, you will drop it. A technique or method always brings its personality to the practice, because all methods and techniques come to us from individuals. Meditation and mindfulness techniques don't come to us from existence - they come from individuals who have practiced them. And because the technique has worked for them, they have passed it along. Now, just because it worked for them doesn't mean that it has to work for you. Why did it work for them? Because there was an alignment between their personalities and their internal understanding of life and the technique, something resonated. That resonance is what helped them stick with it. So with any technique, you have to see if it resonates with you.

## WATCH THE BREATH

Based on the general psychology of the mind, the basic fears of the mind, and the basic desires of the mind, there are a few techniques that have withstood the test of time. One such basic technique is to watch your breath. Watch your breath during your daily activities, - while you're walking, talking, eating, before going to bed, when you wake up - watch your breath. It's as simple as that. The technique ends there. That is the beginning and the end of the technique. Everything we discuss after this is a way to see if it aligns with our personalities, and what changes we need to make in our internal landscape to align with the technique. The method is very simple: Watch the breath.

Now what is the problem here? What is the difficulty? There has to be some difficulty, otherwise, all those people who picked the method would have stuck with it without any problem. But a lot of people have tried and dropped this method, so there must be inherent difficulty in watching the breath. What is it? Let's try to understand the psychology of watching the breath compared to the normal psychology of the mind throughout the day to see where the conflict is. The first conflict is when our mind tries to satisfy our ego. The mind thinks that its primary job is to satisfy the ego - not the self, not your true being, because it does not know what your true being is. It only knows your ego, which is your accumulated self-image. You have accumulated this image over a lifetime of experiences.

Unlike the self, or your pure being - the original nature you were born with - your ego is a collection of self-images put together by impactful experiences in your life. In a way, you can look at it as a shattered vase that is glued together using self-talk. It has no originality. It is broken. All the individual pieces represent something about you. Let's say, "I look good, I am beautiful." That's one piece. "I am smart, I'm intelligent." That's another piece. "I am loving and compassionate" in another. "I'm focused and hardworking," in yet another piece. There are innumerable pieces. They were all separate, but using your self-talk and your ability to talk to yourself, you brought all these things together and created a coherent self-image. Now what happens when you stop talking to yourself? This is a very important point to understand about mindfulness. If you miss this point, when you drop your practice, you will not even know why you dropped it. You will not even know why you could not hold on to it, because this is the fundamental stumbling block.

Your self-image is glued together by conversations that you've had with yourself - and this is the conversation that you have with yourself all the time. There is not a single moment's gap in this conversation, because when the conversation is not happening, the glue loses its power. The pieces start moving and eventually, they fall apart. That is why you are always talking to yourself, even in your sleep. If you were to suddenly wake up in the middle of your sleep and listen to yourself, would you be surprised? How articulate? How coherent? How idiotic your conversations are? And it's the same conversations. You are having the same conversations in your dream. You're arguing with someone with the same level of intensity and intelligence that you would use in the real world. You're dealing with the problems in pretty much the same way, so there's no break in this self-talk. The foundation of your self-talk is your self-image.

What happens when you make a conscious decision to watch your breath? As a practice, it is the simplest of things - I just have to watch my breath. But in reality, watching your breath is equivalent to erasing your self-image. It directly goes to the root of your self-image. The objective of mindfulness and meditation is to drop your self-image so that the real you, which is hidden behind that self-image, can reveal itself - you cannot be cognizant of your true self and a false self at the same time. As long as you're holding on to your false self, your true self will never be revealed.

## MINDFULNESS IS NOT EASY

The first thing that needs to be understood is that mindfulness is not just a simple practice of watching the breath. It is a fundamental shift in the way you want to live your life. It is a fundamental shift in terms of which direction you want to move to understand yourself. If you have picked up the idea of mindfulness because you read about it in a magazine, because Oprah spoke about it, or if you think mindfulness is the "in-thing" to do now - "let me give it a try" - you might as well give up even before trying. Most people who talk about mindfulness have not gone to the depths of it. They've not practiced it day in and day out themselves. They don't know how much it conflicts with the self-image - how much it fights with the self-image. Because they don't know all that, they think it's in fashion - "I want to be mindful." But when they start practicing it, that's when they realize that it's so much harder, it is infinitely harder than it seems to be. And then they stop practicing, but they go on talking about it because it feels good to talk about it. They can connect with their audience. Or, for whatever reason, if they've built their business around it, then they don't have any other option but to talk about it.

A lot of people talk about mindfulness and meditation because it has become a part of their lives - not in practice, but in speech. They have put themselves in the position to talk about it. Unless you are sure that everything you know about yourself is not true, mindfulness will not be effective. This means being willing to go beyond and lose all of your beliefs about yourself. It would be a waste of time to fight with this for a while and then give up. But if you can understand that "I have been talking to myself continuously throughout my life. For the first time, I am introducing a practice that has the potential to break this conversation and introduce some silence in between two conversations." How can this be simple? How can this be gentle? How can this be fashionable?

"My life has been my conversations. What I have been telling myself has been my life. I have never let anyone interfere with that process, because I have never let anybody else have this conversation with me. I listen to my inner voice. Even when I listen to someone, I let it pass through my voice. I repeat it for a while until it becomes mine, and then I communicate. This has been my life." Now, for the first time, you're saying "I have to watch my breath," which means I need to stop talking. How can this not generate fear in you? When you stop speaking - for whatever reason - there is that immediate fear that shoots up, reminding you that somebody is messing with your self-image.

When you're watching your breath, you're not talking to yourself. You're not glorifying your ego. You're not doing something important. You're not doing something that's going to make you rich, famous, or more beautiful. You're not doing something for charity. You're not doing anything - you're not offering your love and compassion to people. You're doing none of the things that you have conditioned yourself to do. You're doing something totally different now. That is the point of conflict. For the first time, you're introducing a new seed called "watching the breath." You only know the name of that seed. You don't know what kind of plant it's going to produce, and you don't even know what kind of fruit it's going to produce. You are only told to watch your breath.

Naturally, your mind should tremble in fear when you begin your mindfulness practice. If you're truly practicing mindfulness and watching your breath, your mind should scream in pain. Because it is being silenced for the first time, it almost feels like it's dying. Although the practice is very simple - watch your breath - the simplest of techniques, simplest of methods, every time you watch your breath there's a conflict because the mind wants to talk about the breath. It wants to think about breathing. It wants to qualify that practice. None of that is mindfulness.

The technique is so simple that your entire focus and attention should be on your breath. Absolute focus, because awareness is a gentle word. Initially, when you say, "Let me just be aware of my breath," you will never be aware of your breath; you will only be aware of whatever you're doing, or even lost in thoughts - "awareness" is a gentle word.

When you're beginning your mindfulness practice, a much stronger word is "focus." "I need to focus on my breath. As much as possible, I want to bring my attention to the breath. And when I'm doing this, I'm stopping the conversation in my mind. Only when the conversation stops do I know that I am actually being mindful, that I'm actually practicing the technique. Otherwise, I have just taken one other idea about watching the breath and added it to my conversation. In my conversations, I'm watching my breath. In my imagination, I'm watching the breath, but it's not doing anything to my self-image. It's not disturbing me."

If mindfulness and meditation do not disturb you, then you're not being mindful; you're not meditating. Relaxation, peace of mind - all that comes later as a consequence of that false self-image shattering. And when the true light of your being shines through those cracks, that's when you will feel relaxation. That's when you will feel peace and bliss - not when it is broken. How can something be fashionable and be so torturous? How can something fashionable gnaw at the very root of your being? Meditation digs very deep. Mindfulness digs very deep. These are not practices you can just keep at the surface, and if you try to keep them at the surface level, you cannot even hold on to them. When you try to watch your breath, your whole universe has to stop. Your mental universe has to stop. You should feel like you are tying yourself up. The feeling is the same. Why do I say it feels like you have tied yourself? Because before mindfulness, you were just taking a walk. Now you have to walk and watch your breath. So if you take two steps, and if you have forgotten to watch your breath, you should stop yourself. Literally, like someone has tied you. You have to tie the knots yourself in your practice. In your mind, you have to say, "I need to stick with this." It's hardest when you begin. For the first three weeks, it's going to torture you. It's going to be painful. You will keep forgetting it, and you will keep arguing with it. Your mind will scream in pain.

At the end of three weeks, if you have been firm and adamant, if you have not given up, and if you have been trying to practice mindfulness, then it becomes easier. Then you will truly know what it takes to be mindful. It's not that at the end of three weeks, you become relaxed and peaceful, and you become like a Buddha. No. At the end of three weeks, you will realize that this is what it takes to be mindful. And then comes your second decision point. If this is what it takes, if this is how it is affecting your understanding of yourself, now you have direct evidence for what mindfulness can and cannot do.

At least three weeks of continuous practice has told you that this is the transformation process that is happening. Then a moment of decision comes: "Do I want to allow this to change this much of my life? Am I willing to change this much of my life?" If you're not willing to, then you can drop your practice. But more often than not, if you have stuck with the practice, at the end of three weeks you will realize that the self-image that is being challenged is not real because it was never yours - it was a collection of words and ideas that you've been repeating like a parrot, day-in and day-out.

## INTRODUCING SILENCE

What has mindfulness achieved? It has only introduced a little more silence into your life. Now, how can silence destroy your true nature? If it is destroying something, that means it is destroying not your true self, but your false self-image. If you're able to come to this conclusion, then begins your mindfulness journey. Then you will know the method, you will know the technique, you will know what it takes, and you will know how to hold on to it. But in the beginning, you have to be willing to endure the discomfort.

Mindfulness is not simply watching the breath. It is an existential transformation that introduces silence into your being - to the part of the mind that has always been noisy. That cannot be a simple or easy process. It will be very challenging, and you have to approach it like the biggest challenge you will ever encounter.

You can climb Mount Everest more easily. You can become president of the country more easily. You can win the Olympics more easily than you can watch your breath and gain control over your mind. As the saying goes, the greatest battles are fought in one place - not in the outside world, but in the deepest recesses of our hearts. Mindfulness is the greatest battle of all. It is the battle against your deep-rooted conditioning - your past, your fears, your desires, and everything you thought you knew about yourself.

As long as the conversation is going on in your mind, there can be no rebirth, no new birth. Whether you are a Christian, a Buddhist, or a Hindu, the conversation is the same. The mind is the same, the ego is the same. You have simply added a few different words to it. Instead of worldly conversations, you are having other-worldly conversations. "Now I am born again. Now I am going to go to heaven. Now I am going to dedicate myself to this." You are still satisfying the ego. Only silence can stop the ego. Only silence can erase the ego. Mindfulness is silence. It is not talk. It is not more talk.

The whole of human history has been only talk. There has been no practice. Mindfulness is zero talk and one hundred percent practice. When you decide to watch your breath, your conversation should stop.

Your mentation should stop. Initially, it will feel like you are tired. You'll feel crippled. You won't be able to take two steps without having to consciously watch your breath. But your priority should be watching your breath, not completing the task that you have picked up. If your priority is completing that task, then you will forget to watch your breath. If you are unable to walk and watch your breath, watch your breath, don't take a walk. If you're unable to watch your breath and eat, don't eat. Watch your breath. That is how adamant and firm you need to be. The natural tendency of the mind is to complete that task whether you're watching the breath or not. Because it's a new thing you're introducing, your mind will be like, "Okay, we can watch it. Let's finish eating first. Let's finish walking first." The priority has to be watching the breath. Breath has to become your whole life. Breath should become your mind, your thoughts, your ego, your friend, and your enemy.

All that you've been doing with your mind, you should also do with your breath. But breath won't talk back. This will be the challenge. You can ask questions, but the response will be silence. You can argue, but the response will still be silence. This is the challenge. With your mind, you get responses, so there's a nice conversation going on. You can fight with your mind. You can argue with your mind. You can play with your mind. With breath, you cannot do anything. When you try to do all these things, the response is silence, and you have to accept that. Instead of running to the mind saying, "This guy is so silent. I'm not able to have fun. I'm not able to have a conversation," stick with the breath.

Because it's your mind, your tape-recorded voice that comes back and tells you things exactly the way you want, it's great comfort. Think about it. Even in arguing, there is great comfort in the mind because it's your own voice. The mind has figured out a way to draw satisfaction out of everything, even your pain. But none of that will work with the breath. When you are first starting, all the things that you've been doing with your mind have to be done with your breath. Just watch your breath. Make watching the breath your priority, not the activity. And then slowly you can watch your breath and start moving toward the activity. Once you have learned how to watch your breath, you will know how hard it is. This is where most people falter because they approach mindfulness casually. They think, "How hard can mindfulness be?" It sounds so gentle - like a cool morning breeze. In reality, it's a tempest. It's a volcano. It is anything but simple. Mindfulness is not a gentle word. It is only disguised gently.

## THE DESTROYER OF PEACE

If I were to choose a phrase, I would probably call mindfulness the "destroyer of peace." The destroyer of the ego. A force of nature, a hurricane. That's what mindfulness is. But it sounds nice. "Just be mindful."And look at most of the mindfulness teachings - it's presented as if it's the gentlest of things to do and the easiest of things to do. No. It is not simple; it is not easy. It is your biggest challenge. It is the biggest bump on your road to freedom. If you're not able to cross this bump, you will always be in bondage. It does not matter what you accomplish. It does not matter what you become in life. If you're not able to fight this battle against your mind and win it, if you let the mind win, that's it. For the rest of your life, you are bound to your false self-image. There is no possibility of encountering the real you. You've shut the door even before you've opened it.

Deeper techniques of meditation, and deeper techniques of mindfulness - they all come later. This is basic mindfulness: Can I watch my breath? Can I identify the difference between watching the breath and thinking about the breath? Can I see the difference between silence and noise? Can I listen to my mind screaming in pain and let it be in pain so that I can break through its prison walls? Mindfulness is not a simple technique. It changes everything about you. It asks for the best of all the qualities that you've developed. If you have some courage, it will ask for the highest level of courage that you can bring out. If you have a little bit of patience, it'll ask for the deepest levels of patience. Whatever qualities you have cultivated as a human being, mindfulness will test them all. It will test your sanity. It is not a simple practice.

## FROM YESTERDAY TO TOMORROW

What is the biggest obstacle standing in our way to experiencing bliss, joy, and life in all its pristine beauty? It's our mind and our ego. It's the conversations we've been having with ourselves, which appear very real, but if you dig a little deeper, there's nothing to it. It is just a mad race. Going from yesterday to tomorrow. And look at your life. How long have you lived? This is the game you've been playing - from yesterday to tomorrow. Even if you were to live another hundred years, what would change? Is there any possibility of something changing? No. You will be playing the same game. Yesterday to tomorrow, yesterday to tomorrow. You had desires when you were five, when you were ten, and when you were fifty, and you will have the same desires when you are a hundred. Nothing's going to change. Do you want to live and die as nothingness?

When life was right there, you were passing through it, but you just missed it. You are so busy, so fixated on tomorrow, that you forgot that there is a now, right here. This is the method that's going to remind you that there is a now. The technique is not so much about the breath or your ability to watch the breath - it is about that decision to be in the present moment. That's what mindfulness is. Your whole life, you've been either in the past or the future. For the first time, you need to come to the present moment. How can this be a simple practice? How can it just happen? You're fighting against the entire conditioning of your mind. You have to expect it to be challenging. You have to expect it to be painful because if you can win this battle against the mind, you will experience a different quality of life - a different way of connecting with yourself. Your walk will be different. Your talk will be different. Your vision will be different. It will open up a new door. The starting point is the breath. That's the method. Whatever you're doing throughout the day, do it in as many different ways as possible and as many times as possible, as hard as it may be, watch the breath. Watch the breath. Watch the breath. That's the method.

# Where the Hell are You Going?

CHAPTER EIGHT

# THE ROOTS OF STRESS

Let's try to understand the dynamics of stress. How does it function? How does it affect the mind? How does it affect the body? What are the ways to deal with it? First, the objective of going beyond stress itself is a mediocre one - "I'm in pain; I want to go beyond this pain." You can pursue it, but it's a very mediocre desire because there's so much more beyond stress. Life is not just the absence of pain. Life is pure joy. Life is ecstasy. Life is bliss. Every moment of life can be a pure celebration. Just because we are not living like that, we are living under stress, it's easy to look for immediate relief. "I just want to get rid of this stress. I don't care about the universe. I don't care about realizing myself. I don't care about bliss. I just want to go beyond this stress because it is crippling me and not helping me to be in the moment," or whatever your objective might be. You just want to go beyond stress.

With a mediocre objective like that, the solutions you search for will also be mediocre. It is not that you have not been searching for ways to go beyond stress, and it is not even that you have not found ways. You have been searching. You have found ways. The whole of life is a way of going beyond stress. Every form of entertainment we have created for ourselves, our engagement with the world, is all about unwinding. Why do you go on vacation? Why do you sit and watch a movie? Why do you go on a hike, or why do you swim?

## THE CAUSE OF STRESS

Whatever you do apart from just sitting and thinking about your worries is a way of overcoming stress. So why hasn't it worked? Why hasn't it worked for the majority of people? It's not only you who are suffering from stress - although when you are experiencing stress, it feels like it is just you and the whole world is against you - everyone is experiencing it. And if it is such a common problem, I am sure a lot of people have searched and found ways of going beyond it. Or at least they should have. Here we are, in the twenty-first century, sitting on top of all our grandest human accomplishments - all that we have achieved in music, poetry, literature, art, exploration of space, exploration of the oceans, understanding the human body, dissecting every small atom, and figuring out what the body and mind are made of. We are living in one of the most intellectually stimulating eras of all time. Never before has there been such an explosion of knowledge, and this knowledge is available to us for free. We are living in a time where if we want to find a solution for something, if we want to learn something, or if we want to get hold of something, we can. We're not living in the tenth century where if you needed to find a doctor, you'd probably have to travel for miles either on foot or horseback. You had to make a pilgrimage to meet your physician. We're living in a completely different time, and yet we haven't found a solution for such a simple problem as stress.

No machine or routine can take away our stress. Most of the things that we have invented in the name of going beyond stress have put us under more stress. It is important to understand what stress is, and if going beyond stress is your only objective, then there are innumerable ways, but most ways don't work. If you truly understand stress, then you will ask the right questions. First, stress is not mental. The mind is where stress manifests, but the source of stress is not the mind. The mind is only the mirror that shows you stress. The root cause of stress is deeper, more existential, and is a disconnection or divide between your true nature and what you think your true nature is - the gap between who you are and who you think you are is the root cause of stress.

That is why those who have found their purpose in life, those who have found their calling in life, and those who have found a deeper connection with themselves, never talk about stress. They're talking about something else altogether. They are figuring out different ways of expressing themselves, different ways of sharing their joy, sharing their love, and connection. They're not sitting and worrying about stress. Who are the people who are worried about stress? They are the ones who are living in such a way that there is no connection between their true nature and what they want to be, what they want to do, and what they want to experience, as opposed to what they are doing. As long as there is that separation, stress is natural, and you can only distract yourself. But eventually, when you come back to the present moment, you are reminded that you are not who you are. You have become something else.

Somewhere in the course of life, it is natural for us to move farther away from our true nature, and that is what has happened - so much stimulation, so much information. Even before we are allowed to choose what we want to do, things are dumped on us. It started in our childhood. Nobody asked us what we wanted to do. Nobody asked us what we wanted to be. Everybody was trying to impose themselves on us. It started at home with our parents, then at school, at work, then in the community. Everybody is trying to impose their ideas on us.

We have not had the opportunity to contemplate in silence, in solitude, about the nature of life or the meaning of life. That is the root cause of stress. You are not stressed because you have a difficult job or because you have a nagging husband or wife - although that can be stressful. The real stress is identity. When something clashes with your identity and is not aligned with your true nature, that is the biggest cause of stress. Stress can never be overcome simply by getting lost in different activities. You can take as many vacations as you want. You can accomplish the grandest of things. But if it is not aligned with your true nature, when you come back to the present moment, when you come back to that moment where you are contemplating aliveness, contemplating your being, you're lost. Fear shoots up from nowhere. And if you observe, real stress can never be traced back to just one or two events that have happened in your life.

Stress is more like an underlying current that's always there. And in certain moments, you see it more clearly. It is not like, "Oh, this happened. That is why I'm stressed." If that were the case, then it's easy to shift that activity. It is easy to move away from it. Stress is such a deep undercurrent in our being - it doesn't matter what we do to it - it turns it into stress. Even beautiful experiences, even relaxed moments, turn into stress because of the disconnect between our true nature and who we are. So if that is the nature of stress, if that is the source of stress, then what is the question we need to be asking? The question should not be "How do I go beyond stress?" That is the silliest of questions. The actual question should be, "How do I know myself? How do I know what life is?" No matter how hard it is or how long it takes, these are the right questions. "I want to know what my body is. I want to know what my mind is like. And I want to know it experientially. I don't want theories. I don't want ideas. I don't want somebody else telling me who I am. I want to know who I am."

It doesn't matter that I can tell you who you are. I'll tell you - you are the whole universe. As it's written in the Vedas, "Aham brahmasmi." You are Brahma himself. You are the creator. You'll say, "So what? What do I do with it? Wear a T-shirt and show it to people? I am myself. I am Brahma." What you need is real experience. What you need is a transmutation. What you need is a real physical and alchemical transformation of your being, not mental gymnastics. You go to a psychiatrist, and you keep on going. What are you getting there? Mental gymnastics. Instead of one person worrying about your problems, there are now two people worrying. But there is no alchemical process happening. You are simply revolving around the problem. Trying to find solutions for stress in the mental realm has never worked. That is why you cannot find a single individual who has come out of all his psychiatric therapies and all his interventions and said, "I have found the answer. This is life." At the most, they've come out and said, "Oh, I understand why I was feeling like this. I found the solution to why I was feeling like that."

But what about how you're going to feel the next time? There are so many different ways of feeling - so many different pains, sufferings, and emotions. Are you going to run to the psychiatrist every time? How are you going to escape all those problems, because there are so many? Nobody has come out of mental intervention and claimed that "This is the way." That is why we don't remember any psychologists beyond a few hundred years - even the greatest and best among them. Most of them are forgotten after the therapy session. A few linger along, like Sigmund Freud, because they have contributed something important to the way we think.

But still, we don't regard them like the Buddha. We don't think about them like awakened beings. We don't equate them with our sages and mystics. Why? Because they have not found a solution. At the most, they have told us what the problem is. The best thing psychologists have done is show us that the solution is not in the mind. The solution is not past-life regression. The solution is not to go back and discover why you were abandoned as a kid. That's not the solution. The solution is in the answer to this question: "Why am I disconnected from my being at this moment?"

## JUST WATCH THE BODY

It doesn't matter what happened to you when you were a child or what happened to you yesterday or the day before; it doesn't matter because you're experiencing something now. If bliss is your very nature, then you should be experiencing bliss right now. Why are you experiencing stress? That means there's something that's stopping you from experiencing bliss at this very moment. That is what you need to address. "What is it that is blocking me from experiencing bliss? Maybe I'm thinking too much. Maybe I'm looking for solutions in my mind. Maybe that's what stress is. Maybe I would be able to go beyond one layer of stress by just being rooted in the present moment instead of in the mind. Maybe the solution is to watch the body, not the mind."

How can the body be stressed? The body has no fear. The body has no anger, no jealousy, no desires. It is an absolute symbol of peace in your life. If there is one thing that is always peaceful, even amidst your greatest of turmoils, it is your body. Your body doesn't slap you when it is stressed. It doesn't pull your head back. It doesn't trip you up while you're walking, because it is not stressed. The stress in the body is simple stress. Too much exertion; it just needs some rest. Maybe when you're sick, the body is stressed, but all it needs is rest. It does not need constant intervention. But the mind is different. Right there, you can see that maybe the solution is obvious. Maybe you are too engaged with your mind. Maybe society has become way too mental. We have become mental. We have gone mad. We have substituted all of our senses - feeling, seeing, hearing, smelling, and tasting - for a shallow, mental understanding of life.

We have substituted all this with one idiotic, repetitive, and non-useful process, which is thinking. Maybe if you can think less, you will reduce your stress. And not only that, you will find something deeper because you are going in the right direction. You're not going into the future looking for answers, and you're not going into the past - you're going deeper into the present moment. That's what watching the body does. What is the art of watching the body? It is very simple. Just watch yourself. Whatever you're doing throughout the day, just watch yourself, not what you're thinking. Not what you're thinking about what you're doing, but simply the movements of the body. Watch the grace of the body. Watch the sensations in the body. Watch the tiny changes that happen when you take a breath. Watch yourself when you're eating food; see how the smell goes inside your nostrils, and how does it make you feel? Where is this great joy coming from? The bliss is right there, at least in mini-packages. When you're eating, if you're able to simply eat, then at least that episode of eating is a blissful experience.

There are so many moments when you can just be in bliss. While walking, you can experience bliss. While sitting quietly, you can be in bliss. While taking a shower, you can be in bliss. Why not? But the mind is so powerful. It has overtaken all these senses, and it wants you to think about your stress all the time. The mind is invested in stress - the mind does not want to find the solution. It is scared of the solution, but the solution is two inches below your mind. That's it. If your attention and awareness shift two inches from your mind to your body, your stress is gone. But the mind doesn't like that because the way it thinks is, "Oh, if I get rid of this stress, then how am I going to accomplish this? Maybe I'm becoming complacent. Maybe I'm just enjoying it too much. Maybe I'm just relaxed too much and won't be able to accomplish all the things I want to."

There is a deep, vested interest in why we are stressed. Our mind is invested in stress - this has to be understood. That is why you're finding it hard to make the shift. Otherwise, what is the problem? How hard is it to watch the breath? How hard is it to watch the body move? It is hard because, in all those moments, your mind is telling you that you're wasting time. You should be thinking about things. Somehow, we have completely confused thinking with problem-solving. Although some problems can be solved by thinking, that doesn't mean that thinking is equal to solving problems. It's a total fallacy of the mind, and that's what the mind thinks - the more you think, the more you're able to accomplish, and the more problems you're able to solve, without realizing that thinking itself is the problem.

Mind is the scratcher who's scratching the wound, and as the wound gets bigger, he tries to give you a solution. The mind is creating the problem, and once in a while it prescribes a solution, and you trust the mind. You never question it - "You idiot. You are the one who's putting me under stress. I want to just be with my body - this is my only reality. Today you are telling me one thing, and tomorrow, you will tell me something else. I have never been able to trust you. Every time I've blindly trusted you, I've fallen into a ditch. Eventually, I had to use my body to crawl out of that ditch." So why not rely on the body? That deep investment in stress has to somehow be overcome. Only then will the shift be possible.

## THE CHICKEN UNDER THE TABLE

One day, a man went to see his rabbi and said, "Rabbi, I have a problem. My son thinks he's a chicken." The rabbi was surprised and asked, "What do you mean he thinks he's a chicken?" The man replied, "Well, he sits under the table, flaps his arms, and clucks like a chicken." The rabbi thought for a moment and said, "I see. Well, have you taken him to see a doctor?" The man shook his head and said, "No, we need the eggs."

That's what's happening with our minds. The solution is there. We can see that we are doing something that we are not supposed to be doing. We are doing something totally different. We are not chickens. We're not supposed to be flapping our wings. We're not supposed to be sitting under the table, but that's exactly what we are doing. And when we become aware, when we come to the present moment and see the stupidity of all our actions, we don't want to get rid of it because we don't want to give up on the eggs. Because no matter how stupid an idiotic act or action is, it is still producing something; there is something to look at and say, "Oh, I accomplished this." That is what stops us from seeing the total flaw in the mental gymnastics. The mind is a perfect mirror of stress, and the root cause of stress is the disconnection between our true nature and who we are. The more we are lost in our minds, the more disconnected we are from our true nature. We are not our minds. We are not our thinking. We are not our desires. We are not our accomplishments. We are in the present moment, and the farther we go away from the present moment, the more stressed life becomes. The simplest, easiest way to come back to the present moment is to come back to that citadel of peace - your body.

# Where the Hell are You Going?

# CHAPTER NINE

# PATTERN INTERRUPTIONS

*You mentioned pattern interruption in your talk yesterday. Can you give more examples we might use to help with mindfulness?*

First, it's important to understand the difference between conscious and unconscious actions. From the outside, the difference is very small. If you were to look at two people going about their lives, one person would be fully conscious of his actions, his thoughts, and his emotions - he's fully in the moment, and there's another person who's totally unaware of what he's doing, he's lost somewhere. Unless you have a keen sense of observation and have experienced the difference between conscious and unconscious action, you won't be able to notice the difference. Even if you notice the difference, you will not be sure if it is significant enough because action is what we are used to, not the stillness that supports it. Sounds are what we are used to, not the silence that supports them. Unconsciousness is what we are used to, not the consciousness that supports it.

Because our senses are tuned to recognize change and movement, we don't pay too much attention to the difference between conscious and unconscious action. But that difference makes all the difference to your inner quality of life. From the outside, life is just a pattern. Human beings are waking up, moving, living, and dying in a pattern. There's deep unconsciousness in our daily activities. We become self-aware once in a while, and even that is a mystery to us: Why do we become self-aware? You might be sitting and watching a movie for half an hour or an hour, and you're not even aware of yourself. You're not aware of who's sitting next to you. You're not aware of what's happening.

Let's say you're sitting in the theater. You're not aware of what's happening outside. You are in a different alternate reality. The world could be ending on the outside. There might be a hurricane, a fire, or a flood, anything that is beyond your immediate perception, and see how easily you can slip into an alternate universe of your own. It is just a movie with colors and lights. Yes, a lot of effort goes into creating the delusion, but it's not that hard for you to get trapped in the delusion and become unconscious of what's going on around you.

Unconsciousness is a natural state of our being - although it shouldn't be because, deep down, we are conscious beings. Why has unconsciousness become our reality? In the allegory of the caves, Plato gives an example.

## PRISONERS IN A CAVE

There are prisoners in a cave. They are chained inside the cave, and they've lived in that cave all their lives. They've never been out. They've never seen the light. In a way, they don't know what reality is. All they have been watching are shadows moving on the walls of the cave, and their backs are turned to the light. They cannot see the light. They cannot see the source of light. They only see moving shadows. So their entire perception of life comes from the way those shadows move. The way the shadows come and go.

They don't even realize that those shadows are being formed, and they are contributing to those shadows because it is their bodies that are falling there as shadows. They can recognize small patterns, but they can never make the connection that there is something more to those shadows because they've lived in that prison all their lives.

Once, one prisoner is taken out of the cave, and he sees the light for the first time. Initially, he's blind. Light, which is supposed to make things visible, blinds him. Why? Because he's lived in darkness for so long. But it's only a matter of time before he can see things clearly. His eyes get adjusted to the light, and then he can see the colors. He can see life in all its glorious beauty.

Unconsciousness has become so much of a reality, has become such a deep pattern, that consciousness is blinding us. Consciousness is crippling for us. That is why when you try to become aware of your actions, it is uncomfortable. It is like walking into the sun for the first time.

Now, how much is the difference between living your entire life stuck in a cave, watching nothing but shadows, and walking into the garden of life to sing, dance, move, and feel life? That much is the difference between unconscious and conscious living. First, there is recognition that there is deep unconsciousness, and unconsciousness is nothing but a pattern that has already set in. You don't even have to struggle to recognize it. Your walk is an unconscious one. Alan Watts says that when you're walking, although you say you're walking, you're not using your hands to lift each leg and put it in front. It is just happening by itself, but in language, we are always "doing" something. In language, even though we say we are always doing something, in reality, most of it is simply happening. We say, "I am walking." In a way, we are saying, "I am doing it. I am making the walking happen." We never say "It's walking," or "I'm going through the experience of walking," or "Walking is happening to me." We don't use language like that because it somehow takes us out of the picture. You want to be there, and you want to take credit for everything that is happening so, "I am walking." "I am eating." "I am sleeping." Even sleeping - what are you doing while sleeping? But still, you say "I am sleeping."

This is where it becomes difficult for us to recognize how much of what we do is pure unconsciousness. Because we use conscious language that is connected to the "I," which is connected to the self, it feels like, "I am walking, sleeping, or eating, so I have to be doing it consciously." In the world of language, it appears to be conscious. In reality, there's deep unconsciousness. These are all set patterns that are just happening.

## THE PRESENT MOMENT

The first step is to recognize that there is hardly any awareness of the present moment. The present moment, for all practical purposes, is nonexistent. It is so fleeting. Once in a while, mysteriously, you're

Where the Hell are You Going?

thrown back to the present moment, and as quickly as you come back, you go away. There's something - it's almost like the two poles of a magnet - the mind is one pole, and the present moment is the other pole. Somehow, our two poles are in the same place at the present moment. What happens when two similar forces come together? They repel each other. So it's almost like when we try to come to the present moment, it's like a magnet pushing us away. We are pushed from the past into the future. And the farther we go away from our original nature - to the opposite pole - we can be there for as long as we want. This great attraction will continue into the future. There's also a great attraction to moving into the past.

Think about it. If you were sitting and having a conversation with someone, which conversation would be more entertaining? Is it the conversation of the present moment? What's happening right there? Would you be talking about breathing? Would you be talking about body sensations? Would you be talking about the sounds and sensations happening in the present moment? Or would you be talking about what mankind's going to be like in a thousand years? What's going to happen to humanity? Or where did we come from? How old is the universe? Naturally, we'll be talking about the past and the future because that is entertainment for the mind.

That is the pattern we need to recognize, and that is the pattern that has to be interrupted. So how do you do it? You can use every tool that is available to your mind and body to interrupt the pattern. You can use your body as a pattern interrupter - to interrupt the movements of the body. The moment you recognize that "it's just happening and I am not consciously doing it," you interrupt the pattern. So when you're walking, change the pace. It's not just slowing down. If you're walking fast, slow down. If you're walking slowly, speed up and try as much as possible to bring your awareness to what's happening. Similarly to your thoughts - if you've been thinking in a certain way, you can observe the pace of your thoughts. If you think it's too fast, slow it down. If you think it's too slow, pace it up. As long as you are involved in it, you are interrupting the pattern.

You can interrupt patterns wherever there are patterns, but once you understand that you are in deep unconsciousness, that life is deep unconsciousness, and that most of the things are simply happening, you can use all that to bring yourself back to the present moment. Every time you are bringing yourself to the present moment you have interrupted the pattern, and you've allowed yourself to change that unconscious action into conscious action.

# Where the Hell are You Going?

# Chapter Ten

# Help me Sleep

*What are some things I can do during the day that will help me sleep better at night?*

More than what should you do, the question should be, what should you not do, because sleep is your nature. You don't have to put in additional effort just to sleep. By its very nature, putting effort into doing something just to go to sleep is contradictory. Sleep is a state where you don't want to do anything, and that is why you're going to sleep. If you still want to do something, why are you going to sleep? This desire to continue "doing" is important to understand.

In your waking consciousness, you are continuously engaging with your thoughts. You're interacting with them. You're having a conversation - you're arguing, you're arranging things, you're planning. There's so much going on in waking consciousness. Although the same things happen in a dream, there's not much interference. A dream when you're asleep happens in a different dimension - it's uninterrupted dreaming. Although it is dreaming, although you're asleep and unconscious, because there's no constant interference, it is not disturbing. It just happens by itself. But during the day, there is something that you add to your dreaming process that makes it all disturbing.

It is important to understand the mind's functioning mechanisms and nature because once you understand how the mind works and what it is, you will be able to identify and challenge your assumptions about it.


## MIND NEVER SLEEPS

When you are learning about something external, you can approach it more objectively because you are not emotionally invested in it. Because you can sleep, you can break the pattern of the mind and shift it into an alternate dreaming dimension. If your mind were to be preoccupied with your daily problems uninterruptedly for days and weeks together, it would for sure go mad. So what is keeping us sane? It is an inbuilt evolutionary mechanism that puts us to sleep. That is what is helping us endure the mind. Otherwise, the mind is hell-bent on driving us crazy, and it tries to do it in every way possible.

Even the simplest of problems and issues give the impression that you haven't solved them - "If you don't get on top of that problem within the next three seconds, you're going to explode." But it's all happening in the mind. In reality, nothing has changed. Your body is the same. The world is still the same. The birds are still flying. Flowers are still blossoming. The clouds are still moving. You are still breathing. Nothing has changed. In your biochemistry, nothing has changed. Physically, nothing has changed. Nobody is holding a gun to your head, and yet you're doing it to yourself. You're holding the gun to your head yourself. This has to make you wonder about the nature of the mind. "Maybe the mind is not my friend. Maybe the mind is a necessary evil. I have to deal with it very cautiously and very carefully. Maybe that is where all my happiness and peace of mind lie. All that I'm searching for has been denied to me by my mind."


## CHINESE WATER TORTURE

Here's an example of how easy it is to drive the mind crazy - how easily we can tip over, lose our sense of being, and be lost. It doesn't take much. You must have heard about Chinese water torture, where drops of water are made to fall on the forehead of the subject. The water frequency is set at a certain level where every minute or so, the water keeps dropping. The Chinese were smart in understanding how easily they could drive someone crazy. Now what is happening? Just a water drop. It's not hot, it's not cold, it's not burning - nothing. It's just normal water falling on your forehead. Why does it drive you crazy? Because it is happening constantly. You try to forget about it, but you cannot forget about it because you know the water is going to fall. Initially, your mind is okay with it - it's just water. Then slowly, it begins to exaggerate. It begins to amplify the sensations to a point where, when you're waiting for the next drop to fall, it almost feels like somebody's going to shoot you. The mind can take the intensity of water dropping on your forehead to a level where it can cause unbelievable physical pain and mental torture. Again, who is creating the torture? Is it the water? How can water create torture? The environment has nothing to do with it. It is in your mind. Why? Because you're unable to stop something - it's as simple as that. Because you don't have control over when to stop that water from falling on you, your mind goes crazy.

Two things drive the mind insane. If you can avoid these two things, sleep is a simple thing. You can easily deal with it. One is repetition. The mind is disturbed the most if the same thought comes back again and again and again. It is a repeated thought that eventually leads to boredom, deep levels of sadness, and depression. As long as the mind is entertaining new thoughts - there's a new flow of thoughts, there's no insanity. The mind can beautifully deal with new thoughts. But where it gets addicted is with the same pattern of thought. If you watch your mind closely, you only have a few specific patterns of thoughts that disturb you the most. The majority of thoughts are not a problem - you can easily deal with them. There are just a few thoughts that come again and again in a rhythmic fashion that disturb you the most. Repetition is what you need to guard yourself against.

The second thing is control - not having the ability to step away. Whatever thought process might be running through your mind, at your choosing and by your will, if you choose to stop and do something else, you should be able to. You should be in a state where you can stop a thought process. If you're finding it hard to stop a thought process, that means you're not watching your body. You're not watching your mind. You're not in the present moment. You're lost in thought, so it is dictating. You want to step away from it, but you're unable to do so. These are the two things that drive you crazy - lack of control over your thoughts and repeating thought processes.

## WATCH YOUR THOUGHTS

Now, let's come back to the question: What is it that you need to do throughout the day? What is it that you can do that can help you sleep better? Don't allow the same disturbing, repetitive thought to keep nagging you throughout the day. Identify those thoughts and move away from them. The only way you can identify those thoughts is if you're watching them - if you're mindful. There is no other solution. No psychoanalysis. No deep-dive introspection of the mind, no regression analysis - nothing will help. Because of all that, you are already doing too much. You're already jumping into your mind. The only thing that can work and that has worked is dispassionate, disconnected, distanced viewing of the mind, where you have to separate yourself from the mind, which is as simple as being with the body and simply watching the mind. When you watch it, you can see the repetitive patterns, and when the same thought comes again and again, move away from it.

This means that you should have control over your mind, not the other way around. Notice those moments when your mind wants to be in control. How do you know your mind wants to be in control? You're telling yourself to do something, but it's refusing. Every time the mind refuses and you accept that refusal, you are letting the mind win. Literally, it is a battle between you and your mind. If you let the mind win, it will disturb your sleep. Again, what are you trying to do? You're telling the mind it's enough for the day. You want to go to sleep, but the mind is saying, "Who are you to decide? I'm still not done. I'm still trying to solve this problem. I can still go on," because the mind does not need rest. The ultimate objective of the mind is to drive you crazy, so it will try to do it in every way possible. You have to deal with the mind craftily, and intelligently. Yes. It is your mind. It is very powerful. It is smart. It is intelligent, and all that. But at the same time, because it is disconnected from reality, it is not in the present moment. The propensity for it to go crazy is very high, and if it is not allowing you to sleep well, that is a dangerous sign that your mind is succeeding in driving you crazy. Watching the mind and the patterns of the mind, stepping away from repetitions, and staying rooted in the body is the only way to deal with the insanity of the mind.

# Where the Hell are You Going?

# CHAPTER ELEVEN

# GATEWAY TO CONSCIOUSNESS

*How can we use the body as a gateway to accessing higher states of consciousness or spiritual experiences?*

Before knowing how to use the body - knowing what to use it for, we need to understand how we have misused it, and why we have misused it. What is our fundamental understanding of the human body? What is our philosophy about the body? The way we look at the human body is the way we treat it, and that depends on our deeply rooted idea of what a body is.

To understand how we have been looking at the body, we have to go very far into the past. There are a lot of ideas that have been passed down, and people have played with those ideas for a while. Every generation has some idea that takes over the human race and becomes popular. People start believing in it and trusting it. Then eventually, over time, people come to realize the invalidity of that idea and move on to something else. But most of these ideas are related to thought - the way we think, the way we think about ourselves, and the way we think about the world -

mostly in the mental realm. However, there are certain deeply rooted ideas about the body that have been passed down for years and have not changed significantly. You cannot get rid of these ideas by just using your mind; the transformation must happen from within, and you must experience it yourself. Otherwise, you will continue to live with the ideas about the body that you have been presented with.

## NAKED AND NOT ASHAMED

One fundamental idea of the body that has dominated the Western psyche is the biblical idea of the body. It starts with the story of Adam and Eve. What happened in the Garden of Eden, to two innocent creatures of existence, blissful in their nakedness, with no guilt or shame? They were living with total appreciation for the nature of reality outside them and the body that was the reflection of that nature of reality. That is why the story talks about Adam and Eve being naked. Nakedness is not just that they were not wearing any clothes. In a way, nakedness symbolizes how existence lives. How do creatures of existence live? They're not clothed, and they're not ashamed. You are in the Garden of Eden, which is symbolically a paradise. You are living in your realm with other animals. You are both part of the same reality. You have come from the same nature.

You are both of the same nature, so naturally, there is no need for shame.

What happened next? According to the story, Adam and Eve ate from the tree of knowledge and became aware of themselves. Up until then, everything was fine and beautiful. For the first time, a human being had become aware of their existence. This was a momentous occasion compared to the rest of the animals, which simply live their lives without self-awareness.

Here, these two creatures, by whatever means, had become aware of themselves. What story do we tell from that point on? How do we interpret that awareness? It determines everything about how we treat our bodies. Because that is, in a way, the birthplace of human ideas - the idea that we are separate from the world around us has been the most dominant idea. Approximately one-quarter of the world is reported to be Christian, so in a way, this idea is still subconsciously dominant in the minds of humanity.

The story we inherit about the body shapes how we see it. Unless we have experienced a personal transformation, we haven't seen the body for what it is: an integral part of existence. This is true regardless of our religion. Our understanding of the body stems from this story because it is not just a Christian story. It is also the story of Islam, Judaism, and other monotheistic religions, which are the dominant religious philosophies in the world. Therefore, it is important to understand this story and what happened in it.

Adam eats the apple - however twisted that story is - to put the blame on the woman and then put it on the serpent. The fact is, they ate the fruit of knowledge. Knowledge eventually leads to self-awareness. You cannot become self-aware without understanding your place in reality and your position in the scheme of things. In reality, they became aware of themselves not by eating the fruit, but through some process of understanding themselves. The story should have been, "From that moment on, Adam and Eve could see themselves as a part of everything around them. They didn't have shame, but now they lost even the fear of losing the body." What happens when you become self-aware, in the truest sense, is that you realize that you're something more than the mind and the body. You start seeing that in all the creatures of existence around you, so you transcend the fear of death. That is how the story should have unfolded.

That is what the story was before religions came and completely twisted it and changed it into something else. The original story of Adam and Eve is a story of spiritual liberation. It's a story of transcending the body and transcending shame. It is a story of becoming like gods and attaining divine consciousness in the human body. Adam and Eve is the original story of how you can use the human body to reach higher states of consciousness. But that is not the story the world is familiar with. The story that we've been told is that after eating from the tree of knowledge, Adam and Eve became aware of themselves, and were immediately ashamed of their bodies.

If there is any monstrosity, if there is anything that can be categorized as the worst possible thing that has happened to the human race - that the human race has been suffering from for the past three thousand years - it is this idea that eating from the tree of knowledge made you ashamed of your body. You had to cover yourself with fig leaves. That story is the birthplace of guilt. Man has never been able to, in all these years, fully go beyond this guilt. This is very important to understand because if there's any trace of guilt left inside you, you would still find it very hard to watch the body dispassionately - you would find it very hard to look at the body as a doorway to divinity because you would still be stuck with the same idea that "I need to somehow discard this body. I cannot use this body." There's no question of watching it, because the more you watch the body, the more you will feel guilt. Because if the body is sin, then where the body comes from is also sin.

It is not a surprise that sex is considered sinful in Christianity. Not only that, it is the original sin - the first sin. How can you use the body to reach higher states of consciousness if you are looking at the doorway to heaven and are guilty of passing through it? The condemnation of the body started from there, and we have continued to condemn the body in every way possible way. This condemnation has taken on extreme forms. There has been religious condemnation - the body is sin, and the body's pleasures are sin. Deny the body all that it is born with, and torture it. Look at the story - God sacrificed his only son for the sake of his other delusional children. In a way, what we are saying is that he was willing to destroy a beautifully formed mind and body for the sake of something else.

## SACRIFICE WAS A BAD IDEA

The idea of sacrifice is instilled in the psyche of humanity, the idea that bodies can be disposed of - the body can be sacrificed. What happens when this idea is ingrained in the human mind? We become comfortable with sacrificing other bodies, rather than our own.

This story takes away the sacredness of the body immediately. Rather, it should have been: "God sent his only son - if you want to hold on to that story to show how beautiful a human body is and how magnificent a human mind is - because he wanted his children to look upon his work, his best child, his son, as perfect in every way, and to celebrate him." Instead, the story goes that God sent his son so that he could be tortured and shredded to pieces.

What has that story done to the human psyche? If God can sacrifice, who am I? I can sacrifice too. Most sacrifices in the world have been made in the name of God: "If God can sacrifice, so can I." These ideas are deeply embedded.

We now live in a different world, where modernization and science have filled our minds and removed some of the religious dogmatism. Science is a very modern phenomenon, entering the human psyche only over the past few hundred years. But humanity has existed for much longer. For all this time, our minds have been filled with religious ideas. We have lived with guilt for a long time, and we have acted out of that guilt and these ideas.

We cannot view world events independently of the forces that have shaped the human mind to carry them out. The idea of sacrifice is the same in Islam, where Qurban is a sacrifice made to get closer to God. But why? How can sacrifice rectify wrongdoing? How can it be atonement for anything, good or bad? How can one crime justify another? God committed a crime to teach his stupid children a lesson. But who is more stupid: his children or the god himself? He must be the dumbest creature to send his son to this planet to get tangled up with the Romans and be crucified to teach a lesson. What a great way to teach!

The human race has become totally hypocritical. We do one thing and preach something else, exactly as God did. In his name, we have condemned the body religiously in every way possible. When we enjoy the sensual pleasures of the body, we do so with guilt.

## BODY IS A DOOR

Another extreme religious condemnation of the body is to abuse it for sexual pleasure, to the point where the body is simply seen as an object to derive pleasure from. That's it. There is no reverence, no sacredness. If you do not treat your body with a sense of sacredness, you will not treat another's body with sacredness. If you treat your body as a means to an end, you will treat another body as a means to an end. What is the direct consequence of this religious condemnation of the body? Pornography. We live in a world where, in both directions, the human body is degraded to its lowest possible status - use it and throw it away. Use it as best you can before your youth runs out and then ignore or discard it.

You have already postponed your search because there is no search. Religion has taken care of that, so there is no need to transmute the body, no need to go deeper and understand it. To be able to use your body as a door to move toward higher consciousness, you need to go beyond both of these extremes. The body is not a product of sin. The body is an expression of life. The body is life. There is nothing ugly in the body. There is not a single cell in your body that has to be condemned for the work it does. You will know its value when it stops doing its work. Identify a part of the body that you want to condemn and tell it to take a break for a day, then you will know how important that organ is, how important that part is.

At the same time, the body is not just for sensual pleasure. The purpose of the human body is to transcend its limitations, not by condemning it or just deriving pleasure from it, but by understanding it. We have never had a culture of understanding. Not much has been spoken about the human body as a spiritual extension of our beings and how we can use it to get back to our spiritual roots and the true nature of reality.

There are some cultures, however, at some point in time, who spoke about it. Hinduism spoke about it for a brief period, before it was completely condemned. At least in the modern world, there are no schools where you're taught about your body. No teacher teaches you how to deal with your desires. Nobody teaches you what sex really is. Nobody explains how to use it to go beyond your limitations into a transcendental reality. Nobody talks about it.

The first thing we need to do is drop the guilt. We need to regard the body as one of the purest expressions of life and also understand that without the body, there is no search, no quest - we cannot go higher, we cannot go lower, and we cannot go anywhere. We need the body to become enlightened. We need the body to awaken. The body is the way. Once we get rid of the guilt, at least intellectually, we should accept that there is nothing sinful about the body.

If we do not treat the body as a sin, of course, the next extreme is that we could start looking at it as a way to derive as much pleasure as possible. That is where awareness comes in. That is where watching the body comes in. When we start watching and observing the actions of the body, we will begin to see that the body is very close to the true nature of our being. It is not very far away. The body is, in a way, an extension of our mind.

There is a beautiful story in the Upanishads where the whole human mechanism is compared to a chariot. The horse is compared to the senses, the reins of the horse are our mind, the chariot is the body, and the charioteer is the self. If we do not control the horses, if we do not have control over our five senses, then we have no say in where our chariot should go. We go wherever the horse wants us to go. Our intelligence has been taken over by our minds.

Overindulgence in sense pleasures, being unable to control our desires, being unable to channel them, and being unable to direct them for a higher purpose happens when we do not have control over the horses of senses. But the objective of riding the chariot is not just to keep on riding it. There is a charioteer sitting there. The whole purpose of the chariot is to support that individual. Now that individual is neither the chariot nor the horse. Our true self is neither our mind nor our body. What does that mean? Only by being in the chariot can we control the horse. We cannot sit on the horse and control it. We cannot jump into the mind and control it because we become part of it. The body gives us that stability. The body gives us a seat where we can sit and control the mind.

We need the body to control the mind - we have to use the sensations of the body. We have to use the pain and pleasure of the body to understand the nature of our mind because what happens in our mind eventually gets reflected in our body, and what happens in the body gets reflected in our mind. That is one purpose of the body.

Another purpose of the body is to try to connect with the one who is housed by the body. The body is guarding a secret: You. If you can see your body, then you cannot be your body. How can you see yourself? It is a simple understanding: if you can observe something, you cannot be that. You can observe the body, so you are not your body.

How do you use your body to reach higher states of consciousness? It is by seeing the body as the connection between your true self and your mind. The body is a mediator between the higher realm - the deeper realm, and this world. The body is your vehicle, you cannot make it an end unto itself. At the same time, you cannot abuse it. If you abuse the body, it will be useless in doing its job of taking you from one place to another, and that is what we have been doing. We have been either criticizing the chariot, condemning it, slowly knocking off its wheels, scratching off its paint - every religious sermon knocks something off the chariot. Religious sermons are a way of saying, "Take away one wheel and just go using another." That is how the body is crippled. A religious body is crippled. Every step you take makes you guilty, so you cannot freely move - you are wobbly.

But if you become overindulgent and make your body an end unto itself, you will forget the mind, you will forget the self, and you will only be cleaning the chariot for the rest of your life. You will give all the comforts to the chariot - give it the best possible mansion. Repaint it every three days. Make sure it is shining. For what?

## YOUR MOST IMPORTANT COMPANION

Eventually, once you see the body for what it is, you can see how to use it. Then the process is very simple. How do you move from the body to a deeper level of consciousness? It happens naturally when you start treating your body with reverence. I would say you need to treat your body the way you treat a bride - a newlywed bride. What happens when you are newly married? Wherever you are, you are thinking about your wife. Wherever you are, at home or work, you are thinking about her. You are talking to your friends, and you are thinking about her. She is always on your mind. You cannot wait to come back home. You want to be with her.

That is how the body should be treated. If you go away from the body, it should disturb you. You should come back to the body. You should treat your body as your most important companion. You are not one, but two: you and your body. The way you treat your body is how you are going to treat everybody else, and that is how you are going to understand the world. That is the foundation of your philosophy of life.

How do you treat your body? If you neglect your body, you will neglect your work, and you will neglect everything that you are doing in the outside world, because that is the primary connection. Let your body be the first and last thing on your mind. When you wake up in the morning, pay some respects to the body. Don't get into thinking, "Let me see how I can use this body," or "Let me see how I can abuse this body." Without any guilt, without any sense of deriving pleasure out of it, just be thankful to the body for housing your spirit. Start the day with thankfulness for the body, with reverence, with love, and with total acceptance. And then, throughout the day, be with the body. Watch what the body is doing. Roughly, in a twenty-four-hour day, we are with the body for not more than twenty to thirty minutes.

That's it. When do we spend that time? When we're hungry, sick, or looking in the mirror. When you're sick, you can't think about anything else. Your body is drawing all your attention. You have to take care of yourself. Those are the moments you're thinking, "Why am I going through this pain?" When you're in pain you are with the body.

Apart from this, when are you actually with the body? Very rarely. Most of the time you forget it. You are in the mind. You're in the realm of imagination. If watching the body is the way you can move from bondage to liberation, from pain to pleasure, from the limited state of consciousness that you're in, to the ultimate state of consciousness, then it has to be the priority. As of now, it is the last priority. We watch it only when we are reminded to.

Mindfulness is about compelling ourselves to watch the body. The more we watch the body, the more unified the connection between our mind, body, and spirit becomes. The more seamless the flow of information between our mind, body, and self, the deeper our connection, the deeper our appreciation for life. Life is not "out there." What we are seeing around us is just a reflection of life. There is only one life - real life, true life. It is happening within us. Our heartbeat, our breath, our desires, our pain, and our pleasure: that is the seat of life. Those sensations are life.

Otherwise, life is just a movie that we are sitting and watching. We are looking at it on a big screen. The only difference is that the screen is three-dimensional. What is the difference between watching a movie and watching life? If we are not watching our body, if we are only watching life unfolding outside of us, we are as good as sitting and watching a movie on a 3-D screen. That's about it. So we are nowhere near life. Naturally, our understanding of life has not deepened. It's so simple. We don't have to go to temples or cathedrals - we don't have to sacrifice ourselves. We don't have to atone for our sins. We don't have to confess our sins. We don't have to do any of that to reach the kingdom of heaven. It is right here: our own breath, our own body, and our own sensations.

## LOOK WITHIN

If there is a kingdom of heaven, it must be within us. That is what that misunderstood teacher said. In his own words, "The kingdom of heaven is within you. Don't believe it when someone says it is here and it is there, for the kingdom of heaven is within you."

We have forgotten the most important thing he said: "Within you." He didn't stop by saying "the kingdom of heaven..." so that we can fill in the blanks. He said, "The kingdom of heaven is within you."

Every religion - at its core, at its foundation, teaches the same thing - "It is within you." Religions transformed into something else because they didn't want people to start looking inside. They didn't know what the inside was, so it was more convenient for them to put it somewhere outside so that people could come to them, trust them, and completely forget about their search.

Religions didn't want people to sit and meditate. Not a single religion teaches you to meditate. They will say, "We've taken care of it, so give us our commission. You go and do whatever you're doing. You struggle, you fall, you get up, and you understand your life. We don't care how you do it. You just come and give us our commission because we have taken care of it."

How much injustice is it to take away the search from the human being by telling him that "we have taken care of it" so that he does not search, and then not give him any solution? First, religion is not giving any solutions, and on top of that, it is taking away an individual's desire to search for himself. Religion has done the greatest injustice to Man.

In fact, in my opinion, religion itself is a form of extremism. It is extremely detached from life. It is extremely far away from life, and it is extremely delusional. Believing in heaven and hell means believing that you will be saved without going through a transformational process yourself, without going deeper, without mindfulness, and without meditation - someone else is going to save you. What a delusional idea! And we have lived with that idea. Why has the world not become meditative? Why is there so much pain and suffering in the world? It is because we subscribe to these ideas.

As an individual, you have to reject all fanciful ideas and come back to existential truth. What is your existential truth? Your breath. Your body. When you move, the universe moves - when you sit still, the universe sits still. You are the world. You are the universe. You are heaven. You are hell. If you treat your body rightly and understand it, that is heaven. If you condemn or abuse your body, that is hell, and the world is a pure reflection of that. Imagine waking up in a world where each and every individual treats their bodies with the utmost reverence, love and devotion. What a world we would be living in!

What is there to fear about another human being? We are living in a world where we are afraid of our own kind. Why? Because the body has been misunderstood, and it all started with that story. Adam and Eve ate the fruit of the tree of knowledge, and they became ashamed. No. They did not become ashamed. They became awakened. The story is different. We've been told a different story. So it's better to completely reject that story. We have nothing to do with Adam and Eve. We go farther than Adam and Eve. It's better to have come from monkeys and apes than from Adam and Eve, because at least they don't have any guilt. They are still free in the Garden of Eden. They're not ashamed of themselves. They're not searching for a fig leaf. It is us. Look at the human condition. It's better that we accept that we evolved from animals so that we can at least look at the body for what it is. The body is the door and watching is the key. The destination is you.

Where the Hell are You Going?

## Chapter Twelve

# Watching Your Self-Talk

*Why do I have negative thoughts in my mind? Who is condemning me and making me feel insecure and depressed?*

Let's talk about how you can watch your speech and actions to overcome depression - a mindfulness technique of observing your self-talk and the resulting actions. When you are not mindful of your self-talk, it's easy to slip into states of depression or feeling helpless.

Depression is a unique phenomenon. In existence, it's one of the rarest of rare phenomena. Of all the species of plants and animals, there's only one that has the distinguished privilege of getting depressed. There is no other creature capable of depression except human beings. This in itself should tell us a lot about depression - a lot about the way we have organized our lives and our society, our ideals of what living is, and the direction in which we are headed.

Why is depression so unnatural? Because it is a learned behavior. It is not an emotion or a momentary experience. It is not sadness, loneliness, or frustration. All these emotions are a natural part of living. Although they can be transcended with a little bit of understanding of the nature of the mind and body, they are a part of life. But depression is unique because unless you are doing something, unless your conditioning and your habits are involved, you cannot get depressed. To even know that you are depressed, you need to tell yourself that you're depressed. Because depression is not an emotion, you cannot just experience it. It is a combination of experiences. It's a combination of emotions that you put together in a loop so tightly bound that you keep on circling in that same loop until you reach a point where you conclude that, "There's no escape. I cannot escape this cycle of thinking." That is the starting point of depression.

When you get into that loop and see no way out, your mind, your thoughts, and your self-talk has to contribute to it. When you are unconscious, without your knowledge, it is easy to fall into this loop - and over a period of time, you automatically get into that state. You don't even realize that you have created this for yourself using your own intelligence, understanding, and the available emotions that are already there within you.

Nobody is born depressed, and there are no depressed children. If you see a depressed child, it is simply a projection of your own depression. You might see certain signs of depression that you identify in you - "Oh, this child is not moving around much. He's sitting quietly. He's not participating in anything. Maybe he has depression." No. You have depression, not the child. You're projecting it onto the child. Children can never be depressed. They can have mood swings, but with one small shift in their consciousness - a new experience, a new place - they forget all about their depression. But your depression is different. You take it with you. You carry it with you - a change of place, a change of atmosphere, or a change of relationships will do nothing for your depression because it is a pattern that you have created for yourself.

## LEARNED HELPLESSNESS

There have been all kinds of studies conducted to try to understand the nature of depression. One, in particular, is important to understand. In the 1960s, a psychologist by the name of Martin Seligman and his colleagues decided to understand depression, how it works, and how we get depressed, so they did an experiment using dogs. Of course, the nature of the experiment is cruel, but we've done it before - we've used animals as guinea pigs to try and get a sense of what's happening with us. Of course, it's a little better than doing it to human beings, but it's still cruel.

One such experiment involved exposing these dogs to repeated electric shocks. Initially, the dogs would fight. They would resist. They would try to escape. But then slowly, over a period of time, as they continued to receive those shocks, there came a point when the dog simply gave up. It didn't try to escape because, by then, it had concluded that there was no escape from this. And after that, the important observation was that even when there was an opportunity for the dog to escape, it did not try to escape. Initially, they had to tie it down or hold it down, because otherwise, it would try to escape the shocks. But after a while, it just didn't care. It suffered without even trying to escape. That is when the term 'learned helplessness' was coined. When you look at the behavior of depression, it is exactly the same. It is learned helplessness. It's not that you're not capable of getting out of those states of depression, that everything has collapsed in your internal and external worlds, or there is no hope whatsoever, but you have learned to not see any of that. You have learned to be helpless, and you have become invested in your helplessness.

This is a very important aspect of the mind that one should be aware of: the mind can become addicted to anything. The mind makes no distinction between good and bad, right and wrong, helpful or unhelpful. It doesn't care. The mind is a creature of habit and conditioning. Once it gets addicted to something, it holds on to it. It could even be depression. Now, this is the challenging part: For someone who is depressed, it is hard for them to believe that they are holding on to depression - that they are addicted to it. They would never believe you if you told them, "You could drop your depression, but you seem to like it." They would absolutely erupt. "What do you mean I like my depression? I'm suffering every day, every moment." But if you observe closely, even in that suffering, there is a tingling sensation of enjoyment that they've gotten used to and are enjoying. The mind is cruel in that way. Once it gets into a loop, it doesn't matter whether it's helping or not. That's what addiction is: a set pattern of doing something, regardless of whether it's ruining or helping you. It's a learned behavior.

There's another example that is often quoted about how elephants are conditioned and raised. Baby elephants are brought from the wild. Of course, you've got to train them. You've got to make them docile enough to interact with them. Initially, they're chained - otherwise, they'll just run away. The baby elephant tries as much as possible to get out of those chains. The chains are strong enough, and they'll hold the elephant. But after a while, if you look at any adult elephant and the chains that they are tied to, you'll be amazed at how they could easily break through those chains. They're using the same chains, but the elephants have become conditioned not to escape, and they don't even try. Because they have lived in that bondage for such a long time, they have learned to be helpless. They have forgotten to look at their situation in a new way. If they are able to look at that chain again for the first time, they'll see, "This is a flimsy thing. I can break through it," but they don't even try. Just that sensation of the chain when they try to move their legs, and the memory that they have tried so many times and have failed, they just give up.

That's exactly what happens in states of depression. You've experienced many so-called negative emotions, one after the other, and you've been holding on to those negative emotions longer. It's not that you've not had pleasant moments, it's not that you've not had enjoyable moments, but your mind is choosing to ignore those because now it's addicted to pain - it's addicted to suffering. It is ignoring all those pleasant moments and is only holding on to the negative emotions.

After a while, every time you touch that zone, just like that elephant touching the chain, you give up. "Oh, I'm back in this loop." This is where the conversation comes in: "Why does this happen to me? I thought I was doing well. I thought I had this under control. Now I'm back in the same place. I've been to therapy. I've taken all these pills. I've tried to meditate. Now I'm back in the same depression. What is happening? Maybe I am a depressed person."

That's where you notice how, initially, it's a symptomatic behavior. Depression is a symptomatic behavior, not a disease. Eventually, that symptom itself becomes the disease because you start identifying with it. There's a big difference between saying "I am depressed" and saying "I have depression." When you say "I'm depressed," there's a way to get out of it. When you say "I have depression," that means somebody else has to come and take it out. You won't make the effort because you have it. It's not something that is happening to you; it's something you have. "I have depression. I have this. I have that."

## FEEDING ON THOUGHTS

It is so easy for simple symptomatic behaviors to be turned into actual diseases. Unfortunately, the medical profession and the whole psychological framework of how we identify and categorize these problems, how we label these problems, reinforces these problems. Instead of moving towards the solution, we make it such a big thing that when you are able to overcome it using simple methods, your mind will reject it. If I were to say to you, "Yes, you've been suffering from depression for so many years, but there is a way to go beyond it in one month. Simple method: watch your self-talk. Watch the conversations that you have, not just with people outside, but within you. Watch your actions. Watch every move." You would totally reject the idea. And even if you tried it, at the back of your mind, you would want it to fail - because somewhere, you've given so much importance to depression. You've spoken so much about it. All your friends know about it - the whole world knows that you have depression. And you know that if you just overcame it in one month with such a simple technique, they might think you've been lying. "Oh, you never had depression. You must have vested interests."

Society has reinforced certain behaviors, and this is not just with depression. Almost all our behaviors have been picked up unconsciously, because nobody teaches us how to live consciously. Unconsciousness is the natural consequence of a mechanical society, and states of depression, anxiety, and stress are natural consequences of an unconscious society. But once you start accepting the conditioning and becoming invested in it, you start looking for sophisticated solutions, grand solutions, and sometimes even expensive solutions. Because deep down, you have accepted that this is something big.

Imagine you are diagnosed with cancer. You are devastated. You tell your friends about it, and they worry with you. You spend days worrying about it and sinking into deep sadness and depression. Then one day, you go to the doctor, and the doctor says, "We have found something new. Here. Just sit quietly, close your eyes, and do this, and your cancer will disappear." You won't even go back to the doctor. You won't believe it. How can it go away? It's cancer. The moment we hear the word "cancer," we know that it takes a lot of effort to get rid of it. This is a general understanding. It's the same with depression and anxiety. We have turned these words into cancerous entities.

They are just simple words - a few negative thoughts that come over and over again in a loop, putting you in a state where you feel like you don't have enough energy to do anything, like you are alone, and like there is no one who loves or cares about you. That's it. But once you start feeding on these thoughts and adding to them, you turn them into something cancerous.

Depression is a simple phenomenon, but the idea of depression can be fed more and more energy, to the point where you start believing that you are depressed. And that is one of the saddest things to accept: "I am depressed." Then you have to reinforce it. Then you have to look for more happiness, excitement, and joy to overcome that depression. The starting point in overcoming depression is understanding that it is a learned behavior. If you can learn how to be depressed, you can also learn how not to be depressed. If you can learn how to get inside that loop and lock yourself in without any chance of escape, you can also find the keys, unlock yourself, and get out. And if it has taken time for you to acknowledge and accept that you have depression, so you should also give it some time to go away.

There are no immediate solutions, but there are simple things that you can do on a daily basis. This is an existential approach, not a therapeutic, psychological, or analytical one. You are looking for solutions in the same mental realm. Instead, you need to move towards nature - move towards how nature deals with all of these things. What is the natural way to move away?

## REJECTING JUDGMENTS

There are two parts to you: the human and the being. The human part is what has messed you up because you have been living in a human society that is sick and filled with all kinds of diseases and symptoms. This is the nature of the society that we have created for ourselves. Until we accept that we are living in a sick society, we will not be able to figure out easier ways to get out of states of helplessness and depression. We will blame the individual, and this is what we have done. This is what politicians and religions have done. They exalt the world and everything that man has created, and if you are unable to adjust to that, they blame you - you are depressed. You are incapable, not smart enough, you need to learn more things.

You are born divine. You are born with everything you need. You are an expression of life. You are an expression of the divine. Who has the right to tell you that you do not have enough education, that you do not have enough intelligence, you are not smart or good-looking? That you are not able to fit in? All of that is external nonsense that an individual has to throw out in order to connect with something deeper, to be able to just be.

You have been living in a society that has made it a habit of adding things to you without you asking for them, labeling things, categorizing you, and passing judgments on you. You have lived so much in this world that now you are nothing but a bundle of judgments. You are not you anymore. The real you is somewhere lost, hidden in all the chaos. Unless you are willing to wash all that away, to completely clean yourself of all judgments, whatever they may be, and all the qualifications that society and people have given you, you will not be able to recognize purity. That is the natural process.

Until now, you have been moving in a very unnatural direction. Every day you have conditioned yourself to listen to people, not to nature. Your senses have become more attuned to what people are saying about you than to what existence is telling you about you. Existence reminds you every moment that you are intelligent, light, and alive. You are complete on your own. Your purpose in life is to enjoy living and to be a unique expression of life.

But what is the language of the world? It is exactly the opposite. It is about fitting in, and they will chop you up to make sure that you do. They do not care, because they have their own agendas - society has its own blind ideals. We may think that eventually it is there to help us, but no. The idea of progress and success that society has built for itself is for its own sake. It is willing to sacrifice peace, happiness, and all that is dear to the individual to achieve that ideal. So if it is required, society will chop off all of your limbs.

If you start to grow wild, if you start swinging and swaying in the wind, you will attract people who will be jealous. "Oh, there is too much aliveness here. Let me put it within boundaries." If you are too excited - you must have some kind of disease. If you are quiet sometimes - you have this kind of problem. If you are experiencing states of negative emotions or are depressed, society is ready to label you, because then it can deal with you - then it can prescribe a solution and build its businesses on those imaginary solutions. Once they make the problem big, then you need big solutions - solutions that take a really long time. You have to go to multiple sessions and multiple therapies, again and again. Why? Because that is the world we are living in. That is the structure we have created, and most of it has happened unconsciously. There is no one individual sitting at the top of it who wants all of these things to happen. This is how it has happened.

When we blame society, we are not blaming an individual. The collective unconscious is what we need to recognize. And if we are unable to see that, then we are not living - we are consciously choosing to be blind, even though we have vision. We can see it all around us. There is no reason for us to be depressed. There is no reason for us to feel anxious all the time. There is no reason for us to be stressed. But if it is such a common phenomenon in such an affluent, advanced society, like here in the West, in America, then there must be more to it. That is another clue. There are parts of the world with living communities where people don't experience one-tenth of the depression that Americans experience. Despite all the comforts, there are more psychologists, more therapists, and more interventions here. What does this tell us? Something has gone wrong. Structurally, we have missed something. We have somehow fallen into our own madness.

The solution is always simple: observe everything. Observe what is happening outside. Observe what is happening inside. Without judgment, just watch. Watch your thoughts. Watch your actions. This is the starting point. No matter what is happening in the outside world, it has to pass through your consciousness. You can guard that gate. You can stand at the entrance of your senses, and you can watch what you are letting in and what you are letting out. This is the only place where you can have some sense of control. Once something enters you, it becomes you. When a judgment enters you and you are not watching, you have entertained it enough. Now it is no longer the judgment of society. It is your judgment. It is your own voice. That is where you need to guard it. How about an external voice? If you pay close attention, you will see that initial judgments are always in somebody else's voice, not yours. For the first few days, you are repeating those judgments exactly as someone else repeated them to you - in their tone of voice, in their style, and their intensity. And after a while, slowly, that voice changes to yours. And once that happens, you forget that this judgment has come from outside.

If someone has told you that you have depression, you need to see this psychologist, you need to do this, and you need to do that - you might initially resist, but after a while, you start hearing that voice again and again. Over some time, that voice morphs into your voice. That is when it becomes really hard to get rid of, because now it is you telling yourself. You need someone else to come in and say you should stop trusting your voice.

Mindfulness is the starting point for observing all of this - all of those external voices that have become your voice. So when you start talking to yourself, pay close attention and see whose talk it is. When did you pick it up? And then, with any new conversations, ask yourself: Is this my voice, or is it an external voice that I have internalized? Eventually, it is impossible to get depressed unless you are involved and constantly talking yourself into it, self-creating that helplessness. By just being watchful, you will be able to deal with it.

## CHAPTER THIRTEEN

# GETTING TO THE ROOT OF STRESS

*Why does it seem like everyone these days is so stressed? Is there anything I can do to avoid it?*

Stress is a social term. It is a polite way of saying, "You're going crazy." It's like you're sitting in the middle of your house, your house is burning, and you're saying, "I'm feeling warm. Why is it so hot in here?" Your house is burning! What you call stress is a symptom of something deeper - something bigger. There is a problem. If you're not able to acknowledge the problem, if you're not able to get to the root of it, then your understanding of stress will just be on the surface. It would make no difference whether you found a solution or not because the problem is something deeper.

Let's try to understand. We live in a world where we don't like showing our weaknesses to people. We don't like showing our pain or emotions. Inside, we could be screaming in pain, everything could be chaotic. You have no sense of where you're headed or what your purpose in life is. You could be trembling inside, but on the outside, you try to put on an acceptable image, and everybody else is doing the same thing. Just watch people, and you will notice that you will not find one person, but two - one on the inside and one on the outside. You will rarely meet an individual. Why? Because we are conditioned to be something other than who we are. Every moment, we are taught to put on a show. Why? If each individual starts expressing all their emotions, all their fears, all their frustrations, and all their joys and excitement, it is very difficult for society to deal with. It's much easier to deal with programmed machines. It's harder to deal with individuality because the response has to be individualistic. You need to understand why this person is behaving the way he or she is, and then you need to respond.

As a society, we have conveniently agreed upon certain acceptable and unacceptable behaviors. When you recognize a disturbance inside yourself and share it with others, when you express that something is happening inside you - a disturbance that you cannot understand where it is coming from, but you know you are disturbed - before you go deeper and start explaining, it is categorized as stress. "Oh, it's just stress. Everybody is going through it. It's nothing new. So don't worry about it. Take this pill. Or go talk to someone, relax, or meditate a little bit." Because everybody is in the same sinking boat, what is the point in discussing the sinking boat, because they know they're in it? If you talk about it, it only stresses you more because you don't see the solution anywhere. You only see the problem, and we have all collectively agreed not to talk about the problem.

Let's talk about the problem. Stress is the outermost layer of disturbance. The real disturbance has more depth to it. The real causes of disturbance are ignorance of your true nature, your body, your mind, and of the connection between your mind, body, and true being, ignorance of your true purpose in life, and ignorance of death. You've been contemplating only one-half of the story of life - which is living, but you have never inquired into death. But all around you, you are seeing signs of death. It is death that is speaking to you more often than life, because life is familiar, you know what it is. Life doesn't stress you because you see it - there's aliveness, joy, and beauty. You walk into nature, and you see life. There's no stress there. Go a little deeper and see what is stressing you out.

## YOUR ISLAND IS SHRINKING

Your philosophy of life is built on an island that is being eroded by the ocean. You're standing in the middle of the island, and you can see that every day, a little bit of that island is being eroded. Your island is shrinking. It is becoming smaller and smaller. The greater your accomplishment, the quicker the island shrinks. How can you not be stressed? How can you not be screaming in anguish? Because in your mind, all your accomplishments and all that you are chasing should expand your island and give you more stability and certainty. But what's happening is exactly the opposite. The more you run around to get things done, the more the inevitable becomes clear - your island is shrinking, and it is not that hard for a part of you to see that sooner or later, you will not have an island to stand on. That is the single biggest cause of stress, and stress is a very polite way of saying it.

It's like you're taking a walk and there is a graveyard there, and as you're walking, you see the graveyard. You know that once you reach the graveyard, you cannot go anywhere else. Once you walk into that graveyard, that's it. You have to live there for eternity. Would you be joyful as you approached that graveyard? Would you sing and dance? Would you rejoice in the accomplishment? "I'm getting closer and closer." No. It's natural for you to get stressed. Observe the root cause of stress. Something is reminding you of the ephemeral nature of the mind and body. Something is reminding you that you have to find something totally different than what you're pursuing now. You've got to make a one-eighty-degree turn. You have to stop everything you're doing and turn around. It is not enough to simply keep saying, "Oh, I'm stressed. Let me do this. Let me do that. Let me do things a little differently." It is not enough, and that is what you've been doing. You've been misinterpreting a fundamental problem for just a minor disturbance.

What you're going through is an existential crisis. It is not stress, because stress is not your nature. And stress is not a momentary experience. Animals don't experience stress. Stress is a much, much bigger problem than you think. Anger, pain, jealousy, hatred, and happiness are all fine because they're a part of your being - they come in the moment, surge, and subside. Stress doesn't surge and subside - it's an undercurrent that's always there. You're being slowly cooked. That's what stress is. It only builds up over time. Unless you recognize the gravity of the situation, you cannot equate stress with any other emotion you experience throughout the day. All other emotions come to nourish you, and even the negative ones come to stimulate you. They come to remind you of your deeper nature. That's why animals have no problem being ferocious in moments, loving in moments, and sleeping when they want to - their existence allows all these emotions to come and go because these emotions don't torment the creature. They are only momentary.

Have you ever seen a worried, stressed-out animal in nature? When you start seeing that, that is when you should know the whole of existence is doomed. As of now, at least you can rejoice in the fact that it's only humanity that is doomed, not existence. Existence is still blissful. Not that there is no pain there, not that there is no suffering, and not that there is no uncertainty - it is all in the moment. But for human beings, it has gone beyond the moment. When an emotion extends beyond the present moment and starts lingering longer than it's supposed to, that's a bigger problem, because what happens when an emotion refuses to leave? A thought arises in your mind. It triggers an emotion - let's say pain. When you think about something that has happened in the past, you experience pain. That pain should last only as long as you are thinking about that incident. Once your thoughts shift to something else, you should forget all about it. But that is not what is happening now.

## QUIT DIGGING UP THE PAST

There is a part of you that is going back to those experiences, that is reliving them again and again and again - the same negative emotions, the same fears, the same frustrations - which you are meant to experience only once and forget. And just imagine the frustration when you are unable to make room for the next emotion or the next thought process. A good example would be that you love food - you enjoy eating. You eat, but for whatever reason, it is refusing to digest and leave the body. Your system is clogged. The food is inside. What happens? Is it a minor problem? No. It is an existential crisis!

You'll have to look at stress from a slightly different angle. Now, what happens when you are in a state of stress? Your entire body is in that state of stress. Your entire mind is in a state of stress. Your entire being is in that state of stress, which means it is not available to experience the next moment. To experience the next moment, you have to be empty. When you're already filled with something, it is impossible to experience the next moment. It's like a cup that's already full. Anything you pour into it will only spill, and that is what is happening. Your emotions are spilling everywhere. Your life is spilling everywhere. It is not contained in the cup, and you have to be very careful because wherever you take this cup you're afraid you're going to spill more.

Look at the way people are moving around. Look at the way they are interacting. They're so careful, and they're always ready to spill. One word, one comment, one remark - they'll explode. They're on the edge. The whole of humanity is on the edge. Nobody is settled.

You might ask, how do you know this? How difficult is it to make someone angry? If I were to give you a challenge - I want you to go out into the world and make someone angry. How much effort would it take? No effort at all. Why? Because everybody is ready for it. They're already brimming at the top. The water is boiling, and the lid is shaking. All you have to do is go there, and it'll explode. You don't even have to do anything. Just go and stand in front of someone. Just stand in front of them - just block their path. You will see the eruption. We have accepted all these things as normal. We are not supposed to live like this.

Human beings can be more joyful and settled, but we are seeing a certain level of stress and anxiety everywhere and have accepted that to be the norm. "Oh, maybe that is natural." No, it is not natural. It is the most unnatural way to live, to constantly be worried about something. It affects everything - it affects your thinking processes, your body, your health - everything. And that is what you're experiencing. But this is only a symptom. The real problem is a lack of understanding of who you are. You've been running a race that you never wanted to run. This is not what you wanted. You have forced yourself to do a lot of things that you don't want to do.

## ACKNOWLEDGE STRESS

Somewhere, at some point in time, you had an intuitive sense of what life was. You had a childlike innocence toward life. You looked at life for what it is - a momentary experience, a brief visitor in time. You are here to play, to laugh, to live. You're here to enjoy life from moment to moment - not to accomplish things, not to gather things, not to grab things, not to prove anything to someone, but that is what you've been doing. Your whole approach to life has changed. You are meant to be one thing, and you have become something else. Your ego has acquired a personality and a mind of its own. Now, your ego is the one who's directing your life, not you. Every time your ego pushes you into action and takes you somewhere you don't like, that's when you are stressed. You're wondering, "Why am I here? Why am I doing this? Should I be doing this? Why did I have children? Why did I get mad at you? Why did I go to work? Why did I do all these things when it is not giving me the most simple, most basic thing in life: the ability to enjoy this moment? What the hell have I been chasing? Why didn't anybody tell me that desires have to be approached with caution?"

Desire has two sides. It is not always pleasurable. There's a pain that accompanies desire. Every desire is a double-edged sword. While it helps you enjoy a few moments, it also severs you, and that's what's happening. You are bleeding. Not one, not two, but a thousand cuts. So many different experiences and all of them have left their mark.

You're afraid that all your new experiences will also be the same. And you know it - there is an intelligence within you that has guided your life perfectly. Your stress is not accidental. There's a part of you that knows why you should be stressed because you've lived your life in such a way that it has brought nothing but pain. Your joy has been momentary. You have to pause and reflect on moments of joy. Your joy is never a continuous undercurrent. It comes and goes once in a while, but worry and stress are a constant undercurrent.

A part of you knows that if you continue in the same direction, there's no point in it. That is what you're observing - the pointlessness, the sheer pointlessness of all your efforts. The sheer lack of sense and direction. Stress is a societal term. You have to recognize it - "I am burning. My spirit is burning. My mind and body are burning, and I'm feeling the heat. I want to cool off, and I am walking in a direction where I'm getting signs that it's getting hotter and hotter. I'm moving closer and closer towards a raging fire. I need to be going in the opposite direction - I know it. I can see all my desires are pushing me further and further into chaos, but I'm refusing to stop and turn around."

Acknowledging stress is the starting point for reexamining your life, which requires big changes - but not in the same way that you've been trying to change in the world. This requires a different approach. Here, the change is not to become someone else. The change is not to improve yourself. The change is not to become better, but to become simpler, quieter, and more like a child, more yourself. The real change, the real transformation that can take away your stress, is you becoming more of yourself. No matter how much the conditioning of society has covered up your true self, it can never take it away from you. It can create a barrier between you and the idea of you. The wall can be thick - it can look impenetrable, but you know behind that wall is your true being - what you want to be.

There is a part of you that knows how to be comfortable in this realm of life. I'm not just talking about, "Unless you become enlightened, there is no way to live in peace." No. Just by connecting to who you are and what you're meant to be, by connecting to your individuality, something as simple as doing what you love can relieve stress. In those moments, when you are doing what you love, you aren't worried about the results. You aren't worried about accomplishments. You are immersed in the process. You are an expression of creation, and when you are creating something, you are closest to your true nature.

## JUST BE YOURSELF

There is no way to get rid of stress other than by being what you are meant to be. This requires introspection. This requires you to look at your life for the first time - to look at your mind, look at your body. First, give yourself some space from your constant thought processes. How do you change this tide? How do you change the momentum of a tide that's moving in a certain direction? You cannot suddenly change it because it's in your own mind. It's your own thoughts. If you try to fight with your mind, you will get lost in it, so you need to shift your focus and awareness away from your mind and onto something more stable. What is the most stable part of you? The body. Once you start watching the body, that is when you realize that the practice of watching the body and the breath is simple.

The method is simple - "I'm just being mindful. I'm just watching my body." Unknowingly, what you're doing in all those moments when you're watching your body is not feeding your desires. You're not unnecessarily distracted. You're not entertaining the same negative thoughts again and again. You're not reliving your past mistakes. You're not feeling guilty for all that you could have done and all that you should have done because you're just watching the body. This is the part that is hard to understand. How can my stress go away when I'm simply watching my breath or my body? When you're watching the breath and the body, you're not stressing yourself. You're not adding to the chaos. You're allowing the water to settle. As of now, your water is mixed with mud, and every time you try to understand your life, you're stirring it up more and more. The whole water is muddy. You want to know what's at the bottom of that water, but you're not able to see it and you're frustrated. Every time you go to your mind and say, "I'm stressed." Your mind says, "Do this. Do that." And you start mixing that water again. You're thinking, "I'm stressed more because my objective is to see what's at the bottom. I'm not able to see."

Watching the body takes you away from the chaos of the mind so that the water can settle down. Once the mud settles down and it's clear, you can see through it. When your mind is clear, it is not clouded by thoughts. How can you be stressed? You are waiting for the next moment. You're waiting for the next experience. This is the first step in turning around, stopping, and shifting your awareness away from your mind and onto your body. And then, as you begin watching the body, something magical happens. You will begin to realize that your body is not as real as it seems. Your desire to protect the body, your desire to nurture it, and your desire to care for it have all been intimately linked to the fear of losing the body. And the more you watch the body, the more you realize, "I can not lose my body. My body is an extension of my mind. My body is an extension of my being. It is an extension of my desires."

By just being with and observing the sensations of the body, you will be able to see that the real body is much lighter and simpler; it comes and goes in the moment. You will get to a point where you can see your body as a wave, not a rock. "It's a phenomenon - I have been living with a phenomenon of life, which is the body. Sometimes it moves, sometimes it's at rest. Sometimes it laughs, sometimes it cries. But I am none of these." The realization will hit you like a lightning bolt. "I have been stressed. I've been worried because I am attached to my body. I'm attached to my mind. This attachment, this deep attachment, is causing all the problems. If I can watch my body, then I'm not my body. If I can watch my mind, I'm not my mind. Then who am I?" The first time you ask that question, a new search begins. The spiritual quest begins. Now, because you are worried about accomplishing things in the world, spirituality is far away. The awakening is nowhere near.

Once you start watching the body, all these new possibilities emerge - possibilities that you could not have even imagined, where your conversations will not be about stress. They will be about experiencing something deeper - connecting with your inner silence and stillness, being something more than just the body. You will see the connection between you and everything around you, and there will come moments when you will forget your body. This is the magical part of watching the body. The more you watch the body, the less important it becomes. Watching your desires only adds to your desires, and that is what we fear. "When I watch my body I might become more attached to it." No. The body is a different phenomenon. Because the body is one - it's not multiplying itself into many others - after you watch the sensation for long enough, it slowly dissipates.

The mind is different. Once you start watching one part of the mind and have exhausted that part, your attention moves to another part of the mind. From one desire to another, from one idea to another - that's why if you begin watching your mind, you will start drifting. But the body is one. Once you watch the body enough, there's no need to watch the same thing again and again, because this is the beauty of watching. When you watch, you will understand what you're watching, and once you understand something, there is no need to keep watching it. Your watching is active only as long as there is still something to understand.

## FINDING ABSOLUTE BLISS

A day will come when you will understand your body perfectly - when you will understand the sensations of the body perfectly. And then your attention will shift away from the body to a center where even your body cannot enter. You will touch a center of absolute stillness, absolute silence, absolute bliss. And once you touch that center, your life is changed forever. You will never be the same again. You have touched the zone of immortality. You've touched the zone of aliveness. And you will know intuitively, "If I can be in this space, in this zone, then I can never experience pain. Forget about stress. I can even go beyond the physical pain in my body. I don't have to worry about old age. I don't have to worry about death because I have found the center of immortality."

Your stress is not a simple thing. It reminds you that you are doing things in service of death and that you need to start moving toward life. That is the bigger transformation it is pointing towards. You've not been contemplating the true life that is pulsating inside you. You've been living on the surface and worrying about death because you're seeing it all around you in every form. Once you start watching your body, the fear of death goes away.

## THE MATTER OF MATTER

Let me give you an example from the scientific community. It is not just mystics, philosophers, meditators, and enlightened beings who have told us that the body is not real - the body is just an imaginary center. Now, even scientists are saying the same thing. They're saying that physicality - what we call physicality - is purely perceptual. This is very important to understand. Up until now, we've been living in a world where we've been told that there are physical things: The body is physical. The chair you're sitting on is physical. The house you're living in is physical. Once you start with this absolute physical idea of reality, it becomes hard to inquire deeper, because you've already accepted that "I am this body." But now, even scientists are saying that matter is mostly empty space.

When we started inquiring into the nature of matter, that is how we started our inquiry into the nature of reality. We wanted to know, "What is a tree? What is a bird? What is a human body? What is a chair? What are these things made up of, because when I hit a chair, when I bang my toe on it, it hurts. Nobody can deny that it's creating a real experience for me. It feels real, and I cannot walk through a wall." That is where the inquiry started.

There are two things in existence: nothing and something. We are something. Now let's try to understand - what are we made up of? What are the fundamental building blocks of life? So we started going deeper and deeper. We started with an overall bigger organism, and then we started going deeper, and we found molecules that made up the body. Then we went deeper and figured out that there is something called an atom. For a very long time, we believed that an atom was indivisible - that there is an indivisible atom at the center of everything, which is the building block of life. This is classic physics - trying to understand what an atom is. And then we started going deeper and inquiring.

I'd like to share this one particular experiment conducted by Ernest Rutherford. In studying the atom - which is a nucleus surrounded by electrons - they started going deeper and realized that the central positive charge, the nucleus, occupies a volume no more than one trillionth of the volume of the atom. This information should make you realize something.

According to the Rutherford model, matter is predominantly empty space. When we pound on a table, it feels solid, but it is the interplay of electrical forces and quantum rules among atoms and molecules that creates the illusion of solidity. The atom is mostly empty - this is a scientist saying it. Scientists themselves accept that matter is mostly void. What are we made up of? Matter. What is the universe made up of? Matter. Everything that appears to you to be real is made up of matter, and here we are saying matter is mostly void.

To put things in perspective, if we picture the nucleus as the size of a green pea, about a quarter inch in diameter, the atom is a sphere of radius three hundred feet, something that can surround six football fields packed into a rough square. Rutherford's model was very much a miniature solar system - a dense, positively charged central nucleus with several electrons in various orbits. The orbiting electrons, like the planets, obeyed Newton's laws. When we started inquiring into the nature of what we are made up of, we got the same model as the macro-universe, because we were only operating on models. What we found at the tiniest of levels is the same model of the solar system. There is a central nucleus, and electrons are revolving around it. Just like there's a central sun with planets revolving around it - both follow the same laws of nature. What does this mean?

It means there's nothing solid. Most of what we recognize as matter is pure empty space. Scientifically, it's proven now. When you experience solidity, you are only experiencing electrical sensations acting at the quantum level. So what happens when you start watching these electrical currents and figure out a way to step away from their influence? Your body disappears as if it never existed. This is the hardest thing for the human mind to understand.

## QUEST FOR ENLIGHTENMENT

Enlightenment has been such a transcendental concept. It's as if it can only be achieved by a few rare individuals. Why hasn't the quest for enlightenment become a mainstream phenomenon? It's not because it is the hardest or the most impossible thing to achieve, but because it goes completely contrary to our understanding of the physical body. When we went to school and learned about the human body in science class, we were taught that the body is physical. But now we are saying that most of what we recognize as physical is pure empty space. If you are empty space, then it's only a matter of realizing it within you. That is what happens when you watch the body.

Experientially, you will realize what these scientists have discovered experimentally after hundreds of years, billions of dollars, so much anguish, and a lot of pain. They have finally come to the point of discovering that matter is mostly empty space. You, as a meditator, as a watcher of the body, can discover it within a matter of a few years, because that is your reality. You are pure emptiness and pure bliss. Your body is just one part of you, and at this point in time, occupying your maximum attention. It is natural for the body to be stressed. It's natural for the mind to be stressed - because you have imprisoned yourself in the body. How can you not be stressed when you are in a prison?

You see a bird flying in the sky or an animal moving about in nature and you long for that freedom because you should be like that. You are much smarter. You should celebrate being a human and enjoy all the modern accomplishments. You should enjoy the fruits of modern civilization and the freedom of life that is unfolding around you, but what has happened is exactly the opposite. You are unable to enjoy all that modern civilization has given you because you have trapped yourself inside an imaginary center.

Watching your body changes all this. How does it reduce your stress? By existentially reminding you of your true nature. It is a deep process. It takes time. It takes effort. Your stress won't disappear the day you start watching your body, but over time, magically, your stress disappears. You will not even be talking about stress. Your conversations will revolve around something different. You will start talking about awakening, enlightenment, and blissful joy.

When you experience stress, even momentary stress, you will enjoy even that because it will remind you of your body. It will remind you of your mind. Once you find your true center, you can deal with the momentary stress in your body. But if you're in the center of stress, which is your body, then there's no way to go beyond it. Watching the body shifts awareness from your mind to your body, and then eventually to awareness itself. That is the transformation. As of now, you are stuck in your mind. First, you need to come to the body. While you're watching the body, you will not experience anything great or transcendental, but slowly, it will reduce your stress. And then, from the body, you can jump into the ocean of aliveness that is within you.

# CHAPTER FOURTEEN

# GETTING PAST THE PAST

*What will being mindful do for me?*

To understand why mindfulness is needed, we need to go very far into the past, because subconsciously, we are more driven by the deep-rooted conditioning of our past than anything else. At a conscious level, we are trying to deal with the mind. We are trying to deal with the desires of the mind and the body. But at a subconscious level, there is deep programming already there that is adding to the desires, which is adding to the mentation. So unless we understand this deep-rooted conditioning that's at the core of our being, we will not be able to truly appreciate the value of mindfulness.

Man is not just a product of his dreams and desires. He's also an extension of social dreams, of religious dreams. He's an extension of every individual who has tried to rule over him. Man has mostly been ruled, not guided. We've hardly had a handful of teachers here and there throughout the history of humanity. They have come for us and stood firm in their love and dedication to help us, living and dying while speaking the words of truth and wisdom. On the contrary, there have been innumerable others who came only to rule, and in that category would fall almost all the kings and rulers of the past - religious people of the past, not the awakened ones, but the ones who were using religion as a way of controlling people. This would include all the major religions of the world.


## THE SEARCH HAS STOPPED

Ruling - having control over Man's mind and body - has been the central occupation of those who have tried to rule us. Unless we understand how much we are a product of that conditioning, we will not know the value of mindfulness. At a certain level, we have accepted this state of reality, this state of life, and the state of society around us as reality. And for us, that is the best possible version of life because we don't know anything else. But what if it is not the best possible expression of life? And even worse, what if it is nowhere close to being the best? What if it is in the opposite direction? What if it has taken us so far away from our true nature that we have even stopped inquiring about the nature of reality - we have stopped asking about the nature of our true selves?

Unfortunately, that is the reality of the world. People are not seeking the self. They are seeking the desires that were planted in their minds centuries ago. In one form or another, we are searching for the same things. On one hand, we're searching for God. Assuming you're a religious person and you fully believe in the teachings of your religion, everything you do in this life is in preparation to go to another place - where all the merits you have acquired in this life will be realized. This is the same philosophy of Hinduism, Buddhism, Christianity, Islam - all the religions.

Their philosophy is that this is a waiting room - this life is not significant. What you do here does not count here; but it counts "there" - where nobody knows. But somewhere, deep down subconsciously, you have stopped searching. Your search was destroyed - covered up. Why? If you start searching for the truth, then what business does a ruler have? What can he rule? He cannot rule an enlightened man, and he cannot control an awakened being. He cannot even come near an individual who's in pursuit of truth because the seeker cannot be enticed with the promises of heaven or the riches on earth, nor can he be threatened with death.

A ruler is pretending to be the truth. He wants that power, he wants that control, but he doesn't have the realization. He wants to be the king. He wants to sit on the throne, but it's all imaginary. Where did he acquire that from? His father was probably a king, and he passed it on to him. Now he wants to rule over the people as a king. But he doesn't understand what people need - he doesn't even understand what he needs. These were the people who were the highest authority figures, whose words were taken literally. Naturally, they didn't want people to search for themselves, and the same has continued today.

Who is asking you to search for your true self? Is your church or your temple priest asking you to search for your true self? Is your teacher in your school or college asking you? How about the politician you vote for once every four years - is he asking you to search for your true self? Who is asking you to search for your true self? Nobody, because they are not interested in your true self. They're not even interested in their own true selves.

It is through sheer chance that an individual finds the path to truth by detaching himself from the world, society, and conditioning. Once in a while, he succeeds. That is why the world is the way it is: so much pain and suffering, chaos, and uncertainty at every level.

We can see this at the level of the family, where misunderstandings abound. The same is true of the community and society as a whole. At the end of the day, the whole world is one family. The individual family you belong to is simply a microcosm of the larger family. What happens at the family level eventually manifests on a larger scale.

Within every home, within every family, if people were to be living in peace, in bliss, being rooted in the moment, and being in love connected to their true nature, we would not see the world the way it is now. We would be living in a completely different world - a different reality. The world is the way it is because we have somehow been diverted away from our search. We have been moved as far away from our true selves as possible, to the point where even an inquiry seems odd.

What is mindfulness? Mindfulness is not a new skill that we need to acquire. It is not something that has to be added. Mindfulness is about being here, being in the present moment, and being as close as possible to the seat of life, where life is flowering and fruiting every moment. It is to be close to nature.

## LEARNING TO BE

Because of all this deep-rooted conditioning, it has become a big challenge to just be. Consciously, we might be pursuing our dreams. We might be fully convinced that "This is my life. This is my dream. This is my desire," but if you scratch the surface of those dreams, if you dig a little deeper, you will see it's stacked upon all the misguided dreams and desires of the past - people who came before you with all these ideologies, pursuing wealth, pursuing name and fame, becoming rich and successful, becoming something important. That conditioning is what we are pursuing. And if that conditioning is wrong or flawed - stress, anxiety, uncertainty, and fear are the natural consequences.

We don't have to go far to know that's the reality. The conditioning has been wrong. The dreams and desires passed on have been wrong. How do we know? The state of the world. How many people can you say are completely satisfied? Are peaceful? Are joyful and waking up each day with a new sense of joy and enthusiasm for life? Are living as expressions of life as they are meant to be, as individuals and as forces of nature? None. Why? Because we are all swirling in the same dreaming and desiring process, which is not our own. That is the most important thing to understand. It does not come from our inner being. It has been added to our list, and that's why there's enormous effort involved - it doesn't come naturally.

All that we are trying to pursue in the world doesn't come naturally to us, but we are struggling to achieve, because if we are not running and chasing those dreams and desires, our lives have no meaning and purpose, since that is our conditioning. Nobody has told us that there are other things we can pursue, there are deeper, more meaningful things. When an individual begins to search for truth, when he begins to search for a natural connection with life and himself, mindfulness is an extension - a simple extension.

What is it that mindfulness can give you? The ability to be in the present moment can wash you clean of centuries of all the dirt and grime that is sticking to you, that has weighed you down. Every step you take, you are carrying all this. It has become thick - so thick it's hard to even see your own skin. But it is there. You know you're there. You know you're alive. You know you're not dead.

Despite all the problems and nonsense that is going on in the world, that aliveness within you is pulsating. It's looking for love, connection, goodness, or simplicity - just to be able to experience that one moment when you can breathe freely without worrying about tomorrow or yesterday. If you can experience one day with no desire for tomorrow, no worries about yesterday - only then will you know what a spectacular phenomenon life is, what a gift life is, what a blessing life is, and what pure joy and ecstasy life is!

We have gone so far away from all this. Now, life is not about ecstasy. It's about survival. It's not about joy. It's about identity. It's not about self-discovery but about self-preservation. Our mind has been diverted in a completely different direction, so we are not even looking in the right direction.

Mindfulness will first make you aware of your deep-rooted conditioning. Although the conditioning comes from the past, it's all right here. Your mind is where it all comes from and lands. Your mind is the screen on which everything lands. When you are mindful of your body and mind and you start watching your thoughts, for the first time you will know which are your thoughts and which are simply a part of your conditioning. You will be surprised that most of your desires are not even yours. Nobody even asked your permission before putting those desires in your mind. You never asked before acquiring them.

As a process of growing up, because you were young, you were impressionable, because you didn't have your own understanding of life to question things, wherever you went, people added their stuff to your mind. It started at home, then at school, in society, at the workplace - everywhere - people just kept on adding. For the first time, you can become aware of all that has been added to you so that you can make choices about what is yours and what is not yours, what is essential for you and what is not essential, what is required and what is not required, and most importantly, what is you and what is not you.

Once you identify this, then begins the process of moving closer and closer toward all those things that you can recognize as yours - all the best qualities of life - connection with silence, stillness, love, and connection with the present moment, which is your original nature. You will start moving toward those - not as a solution to some problem, but as a natural joy. Just like a child gravitates toward beautiful and exciting things, you will start moving toward them.

Once you start observing your mind from the present moment as an outsider, not being involved in the mind, then you can discriminate between right and wrong, good and bad. Mindfulness is one of the most important limbs of yoga. Mindfulness is not just a modern practice - the word is modern. In ancient Hindu scriptures, it is called 'Smriti.' In Buddhist scripture, it is called 'Sati.' These are both ancient practices - the ability to be in the present moment.

Smriti means "remembering yourself at all times." It's fundamental to yogic transcendence and to attaining transcendence of the mind and the body. It's also fundamental to experiencing inner bliss, because if you're not remembering yourself, then you're just lost in your mind. Mindfulness is all about being in the present moment and remembering yourself. Every time you watch your body or your thoughts, you're remembering yourself and your true nature - not intellectually, but existentially, you're remembering yourself. "This is me. This is who I am."

What can mindfulness do? Put the question another way. What is it that it cannot do? What is it that it cannot give? All that the world cannot give, mindfulness can give. All that the world has promised you and failed to give you, you will get in mindfulness. All that people have been promising - the glories of heaven, somebody taking care of you - are false promises that will never become reality.

And look at the beauty of that trick. For you to even know whether these things are true or not, you have to die. And when you die, who the hell is going to know? You're gone. To know if there is a heaven, you have to die. And what is known after dying? You see the whole problem with the way we are approaching bliss. Ultimately, what is it that we are searching for?

What is the promise of heaven, if not for a deep experience of bliss?

There is a space where we can live without pain and suffering. That is what bliss is, and that is what all the religions have been promising. That is what the pursuit of material wealth is, and that is what the pursuit of name and fame is - so that you can feel safe and secure in that space. We're searching for the same thing but in the wrong places.

Mindfulness is the right place to begin, because it cuts out all that clutter and nonsense, brings you back to the present moment, and says, "What the hell are you searching for outside?" Do you think existence is a miser to put the most precious things outside of you? Why would it put it outside of you? You are an expression of life. So whatever you're searching for has to be within you. How can it be outside? How can you be so easily fooled into believing that the best of what you're searching for is somewhere outside? And where is this outside, except in a spatial imaginary dimension?

Tomorrow is purely imaginary. Heaven is purely imaginary. In this pursuit of tomorrow, you have completely forgotten the now. You have completely forgotten that this is it - this moment is everything. If you cannot find what you're looking for in this moment, you will not find it in the next moment because the next moment never comes. It has never come. Show me the person who has experienced the next moment. Show me the person who will experience tomorrow. They've only spoken about it. We can only speak about tomorrow, but we can only live in the present. Only in the now.

Mindfulness is the door that opens the now so that you can wash off all that filth and unwanted nonsense and enter fresh and clean into the experience of your pure being. From there, whatever you experience is your own. The bliss, the relaxation, whatever you find, it's your own, and you will not regret having found that because it's your nature. Anything that's your nature has to be the best of things. At least that much you can trust existence - that deep at the center, at the core of your being, it has placed the best of things. Mindfulness is a way to get there.

# About Avi

Born and raised in India, Avi's professional journey in the corporate world began soon after he graduated from college. However, at the age of 24, he recognized an emptiness within that material success could never satisfy. Yearning for inner tranquility and a sense of purpose, he made the courageous decision to move away from home, leave his job, and embark on a dedicated pursuit of meditation.

Devoting himself to intense meditation for three years, Avi underwent a profound spiritual awakening that forever transformed his life. Driven by this newfound realization, he eagerly began sharing his experience through various programs and retreats. In 2017, he traveled to America and intuitively knew that he had found a place to sow the seeds of consciousness and awareness.

Currently, Avi resides and teaches in Tennessee, where the first Nirvana meditation center is being developed. He speaks twice a day, and his talks are recorded and transcribed by his students, which are ultimately compiled into books for publication.

Nirvana Foundation is a nonprofit spiritual community providing individuals with an opportunity to explore the realms of meditation and self-awareness through books and programs.

Visit www.nirvana.foundation to learn more about Avi and his vision.

# BOOKS BY AVI

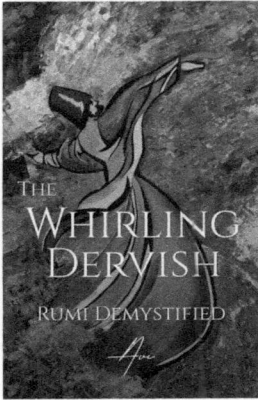

ISBN: 978-1962685009

ISBN: 979-8852311207

ISBN: 979-8392250196

ISBN: 979-8374196740

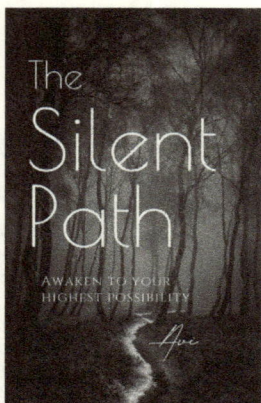

The
Silent
Path

AWAKEN TO YOUR
HIGHEST POSSIBILITY

ISBN: 978-0578637068

www.ingramcontent.com/pod-product-compliance
Lightning Source LLC
Chambersburg PA
CBHW031951080426
42735CB00007B/351